THE LEGO® BUILD-IT BOOK
MORE AMAZING VEHICLES

The LEGO® Build-It Book, Vol. 2: More Amazing Vehicles.
Copyright © 2013 by Nathanaël Kuipers and Mattia Zamboni.

Printed in China

First printing

17 16 15 14 13   1 2 3 4 5 6 7 8 9

ISBN-10: 1-59327-513-7
ISBN-13: 978-1-59327-513-6

Publisher: William Pollock
Production Editor: Riley Hoffman
Model Design: Nathanaël Kuipers
Cover and Interior Design: Mattia Zamboni
Cartoon Illustration: Pasquale D'Silva
Developmental Editor: Tyler Ortman
Proofreader: Paula L. Fleming

For information on distribution, translations, or bulk sales,
please contact No Starch Press, Inc. directly:

No Starch Press, Inc.
38 Ringold Street, San Francisco, CA 94103
phone: 415.863.9900; fax: 415.863.9950; info@nostarch.com; www.nostarch.com

Library of Congress Cataloging-in-Publication Data

Kuipers, Nathanaël.
  The LEGO build-it book. Amazing vehicles / Nathanaël Kuipers, Mattia Zamboni.
    pages cm
  ISBN-13: 978-1-59327-503-7
  ISBN-10: 1-59327-503-X
  1. Motor vehicles--Models. 2. LEGO toys. I. Zamboni, Mattia. II. Title. III. Title: Amazing vehicles.
  TL237.K85 2013
  629.22'1--dc23
                          2013005960

Production Date: 06/14/2013
Plant & Location: Printed by Everbest Printing (Guangzhou, China), Co. Ltd
Job / Batch #: 114804

THE LEGO® BUILD-IT BOOK
MORE AMAZING VEHICLES

Nathanaël Kuipers – Mattia Zamboni

no starch
press

About the authors

Nathanaël Kuipers
Model Designer

Nathanaël Kuipers is a Dutch design professional who worked for several years as a product developer for the LEGO Group in Denmark, where he was mainly responsible for engineering LEGO Technic models. He is the mastermind behind models like #8261, #8271, #8272, #8292, and #8674. He has also collaborated on the creation of many other models. Check out his work at *http://www.nkubate.com/*.

Mattia Zamboni
Graphic Artist

Mattia Zamboni is a fan of graphic design, photography, and LEGO, and he has a degree in electrical engineering. Based in Switzerland, he pursues his passion for graphic design, showcasing his talents within the world of 3D computer graphic arts. Check out his work at *http://www.brickpassion.com/*.

Acknowledgments

From Nathanaël:

Once again I'd first like to thank Mattia Zamboni for his passion and devotion during this project. Without his help, this book would never have reached this high level of quality, which is far superior to what I could have achieved myself. I'd also like to thank the LEGO Group for their fantastic toy and for giving me the opportunity of a lifetime: to design several official models, which taught me so much about how to create a good build.

Furthermore I thank my family, because they have always supported me, my ideas, and my passion for the brick; my dearest friends for their words of encouragement; and everyone at No Starch Press for their enthusiasm and cooperation, and for sharing their excitement for this project.

And of course, a big "Thank you!" to all the fans who have shown an interest in my work over the years. Your appreciative words help me continue to build and share my creations!

From Mattia:

A huge thanks to Nelson Painço for being such a great mentor in 3D graphics and for his outstanding help promoting this book. I would also like to thank my son, Leonardo, who has meticulously tested all the building instructions despite his young age, and my sweet wife, Fabiola, who has actively contributed to this project with her unconditional support.

Special thanks go to Pasquale D'Silva for kindly providing the quirky character for this book. In addition I thank my friends, who helped out wholeheartedly with the book promotion, and the whole No Starch Press crew for the fantastic and pleasant teamwork.

And of course I must thank my greatest inspiration, Nathanaël, who has amazed me with his models and made me believe in an idea like no one before!

About the book

'Just imagine!"

Sometimes it's not as easy as it sounds, is it? Well, help is on the way. In this book you'll find the secrets of a true master builder—so be prepared for some pretty advanced techniques.

Because we don't want to bore you with theory, our focus is on building in practice, guiding you with step-by-step instructions. By creatively using the same pieces in 10 different configurations, you'll see the amazing potential of the LEGO brick.

We hope that this book helps you to discover the many possibilities that the LEGO system has to offer, unleashing your creativity and inspiring you to create your own original models!

What you need

Every project in this book uses a common set of pieces—a complete list is shown in the Bill of Materials on the facing page. If you have set #5867, the LEGO CREATOR Super Speedster, you have all the bricks you need.

If you have a collection of other LEGO sets and want to determine which pieces you're missing from set #5867, we recommend using Rebrickable (*http://rebrickable. com/*). To buy the parts you're missing, you have a few options.

If you're not lucky enough to live near an official LEGO retail store with a "Pick a Brick" wall, you can buy individual pieces online (*http://shop.lego.com/en-US/ Pick-A-Brick-ByTheme*). You can also buy LEGO pieces from BrickLink (*http://www. bricklink.com/*), a comprehensive, international marketplace for buying new and used bricks.

Don't forget that you can use parts in different colors or with similar shapes, too. That's what's so cool about building with LEGO bricks! You can always redesign

3x
3x
11x
7x
2x
2x
2x
2x
8x
2x
4x
1x
1x
4x
2x
2x

3x
2x
4x
3x
1x
5x
1x
1x
8x
1x
2x
3x
2x
2x
1x
2x
3x
1x

4x

17x
2x
4x
4x
2x
2x
4x
6x
4x
1x
2x
2x
2x
2x
2x
4x
5x
2x
4x
2x

3x
2x
2x
1x
2x
1x
5x
1x
2x
2x
2x
2x
4x
3x

4x
3x
2x
1x
1x
1x

3x
3x

4x
4x
6x
1x
6x
4x
2x
1x
6x
4x
4x
1x

1x
4x
2x
2x
6x
2x
3x

THESE ARE THE PARTS
USED TO CREATE THE
MODELS IN THIS BOOK.
IF YOU ARE MISSING
A FEW PIECES, DON'T
WORRY! BE CREATIVE
AND REPLACE THEM
WITH SOMETHING
SIMILAR OR BUILD IN
A DIFFERENT COLOR!

//CONTENTS

FOR EACH MODEL IN THIS BOOK, YOU'LL FIND A CLASSIFICATION LIKE THIS ON THE FIRST PAGE. THIS TELLS YOU HOW COMPLEX THE MODEL IS.

HOW DIFFICULT THE MODEL IS TO BUILD ⎯

HOW MANY WORKING FUNCTIONS IT HAS ⎯

HOW MANY PIECES ARE NEEDED ⎯

Complexity
Functions
Pieces

THE COMPLEXITY SCORE IS BASED ON THE BUILDING TECHNIQUES THAT ARE USED IN THE MODEL. CHECK OUT "BUILDING TRICKS" ON THE NEXT PAGE TO LEARN MORE ABOUT THESE TECHNIQUES.

FROM EASY...

TO ADVANCED!

BUILDING TRICKS

A Quick Refresher

Just to refresh your memory, here's a quick overview of some ideas we covered in Volume 1 of The LEGO Build-It Book.

The length and width of LEGO elements are measured in STUDS. The height of a piece can be measured in units of BRICKS or PLATES.

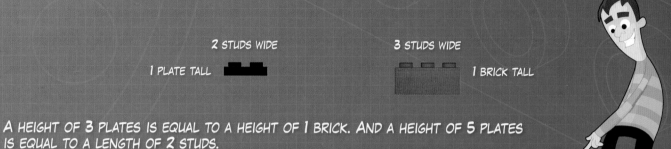

2 STUDS WIDE

1 PLATE TALL

3 STUDS WIDE

1 BRICK TALL

A height of 3 plates is equal to a height of 1 brick. And a height of 5 plates is equal to a length of 2 studs.

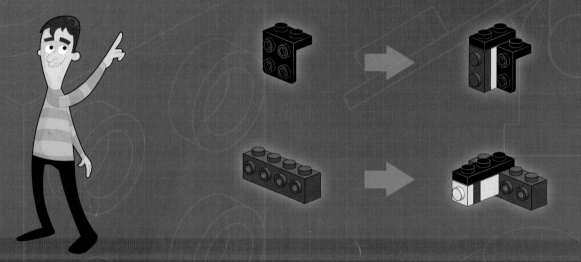

3 PLATES = 1 BRICK

5 PLATES = 2 STUDS

The "magic formula" of 5 plates = 2 studs becomes particularly important when you're building sideways.

You can use these techniques to make a VERTICAL REINFORCEMENT...

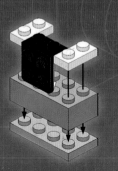
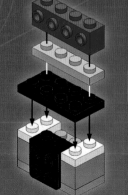
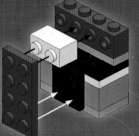
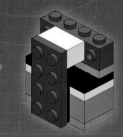

That's so cool!

OR EVEN BUILD UPSIDE DOWN!

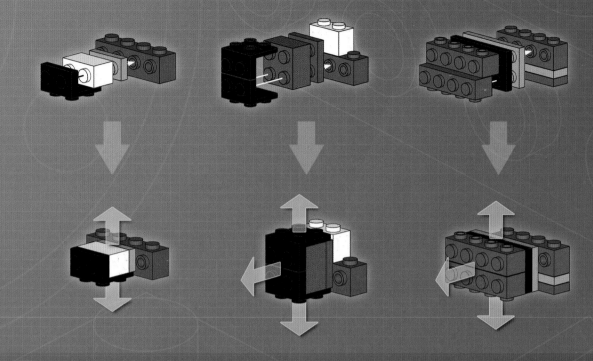

TO MAKE THINGS EVEN MORE EXCITING, YOU CAN MIX THOSE SIDEWAYS BUILDING TECHNIQUES WITH HINGES, JOINTS, AND PINS. THIS LETS YOU CREATE PRETTY MUCH ANY TYPE OF ARTICULATION AND BUILD IN ALMOST ANY DIRECTION!

360° RANGE

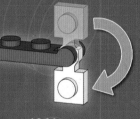

180° RANGE

90° RANGE

IF YOUR HEAD IS SPINNING, DON'T WORRY. THIS BOOK IS FILLED WITH LOADS OF EXAMPLES, PUTTING ALL THIS THEORY INTO PRACTICE.

HERE'S A HINT: CHECK OUT THE CONSTRUCTION ON THE FRONT OF THE HOT ROD AND THE FOREFORK OF THE CHOPPER WHILE YOU'RE BUILDING.

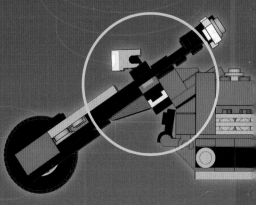

NOW THAT YOU KNOW HOW TO BUILD IN DIFFERENT DIRECTIONS, YOU MIGHT START LOOKING AT YOUR LEGO PIECES IN A WHOLE NEW LIGHT. DEPENDING ON ITS ORIENTATION, A PIECE CAN NOW REPRESENT A MULTITUDE OF DIFFERENT DETAILS. LET'S TAKE ONE PIECE AS AN EXAMPLE.

HERE'S A BAR IN ITS NORMAL, UPRIGHT POSITION, AS STRUCTURAL REINFORCEMENT FOR THE WRECKER'S BOOM. SIMPLE ENOUGH.

BUT WHEN WE FLIP IT SIDEWAYS, IT CAN BECOME AN AIR INTAKE ON THE SIDE OF THE F1 RACER.

OR WE CAN FLIP IT FORWARD, TURNING IT INTO THE BUMPER ON THE DUNE BUGGY.

WHEN COMBINED WITH A CLIP, IT CAN EVEN BE USED AS A FUNCTIONAL ELEMENT, LIKE THE SUPPORT FOR THE BLADE ON THE EXCAVATOR.

PRETTY NEAT. JUST ONE ELEMENT HAS A TON OF DIFFERENT USES. NOW LET'S START BUILDING!

Complexity
Functions
Pieces

HOT ROD

Design notes: chop top, exposed V8 engine, big exhaust pipes, wide rear axle

Technical specifications:

Dimensions (l × w × h):	18 × 10 × 8 studs
Wheelbase:	13 studs
Axle width front/rear:	8/10 studs

Features: opening doors

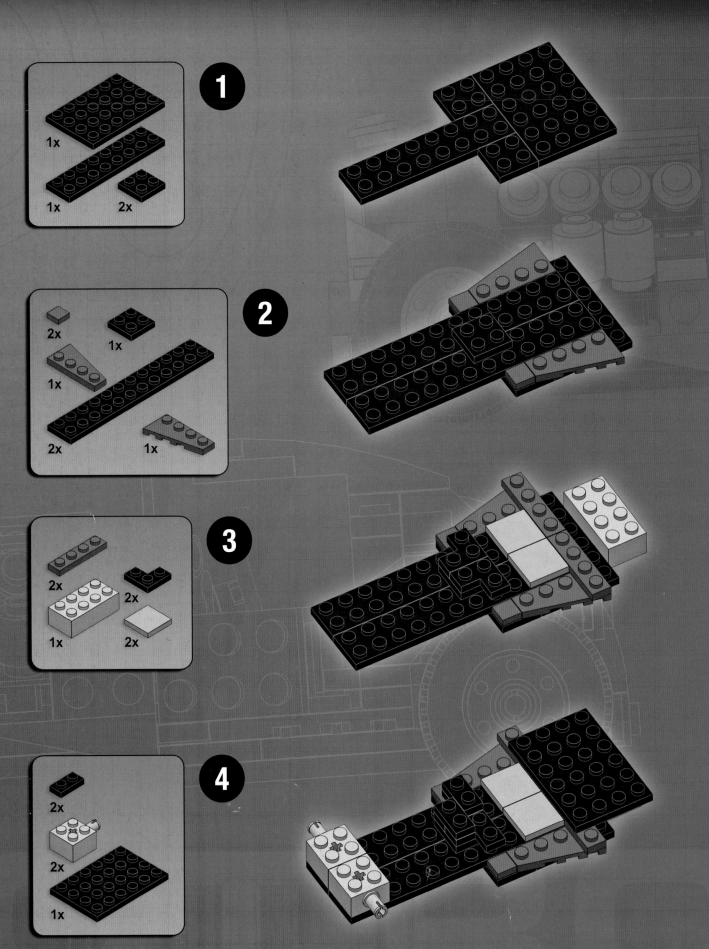

1

1x
1x 2x

2

2x
1x
1x
2x 1x

3

2x
2x
1x 2x

4

2x
2x
1x

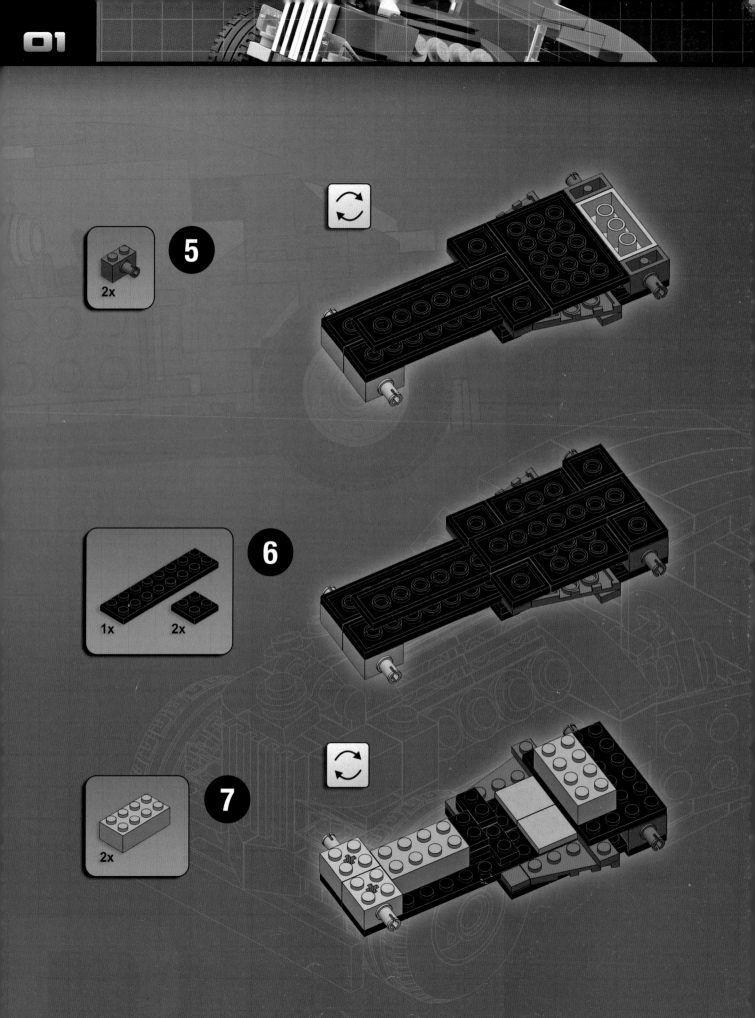

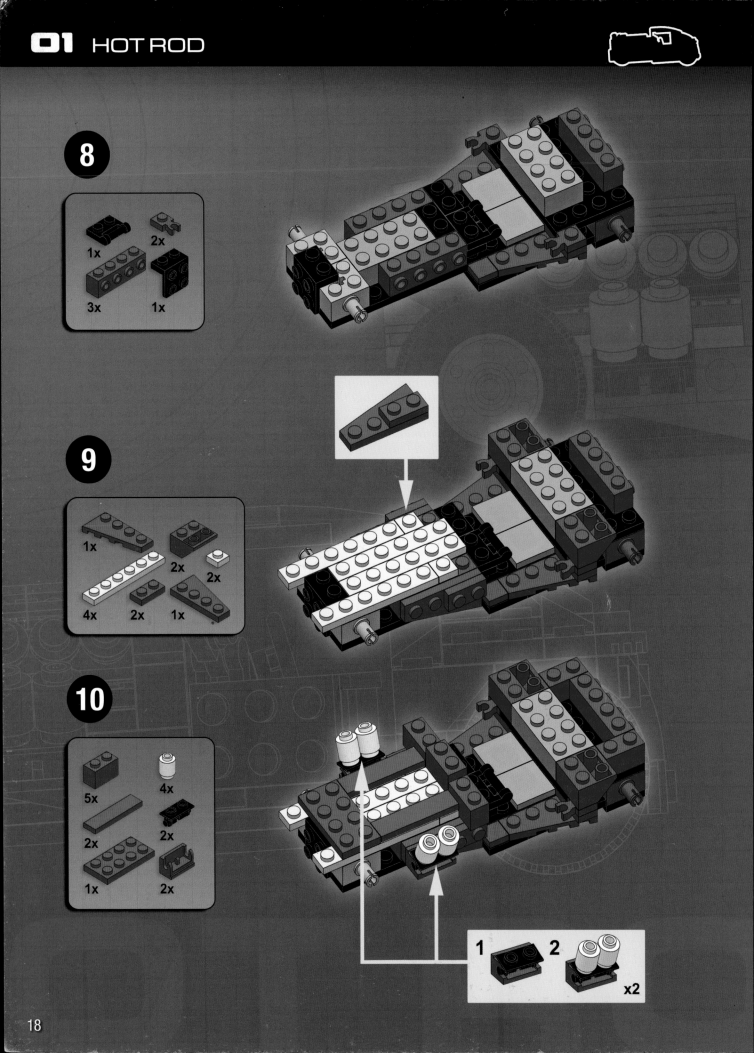

8

1x   2x

3x   1x

9

1x

2x   2x

4x   2x   1x

10

5x   4x

2x   2x

1x   2x

1   2   x2

11

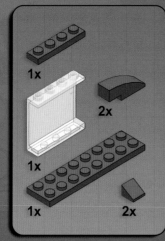

1x
1x
2x
1x
2x

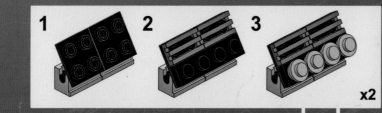

1   2   3   x2

12

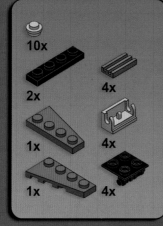

10x
2x   4x
1x   4x
1x   4x

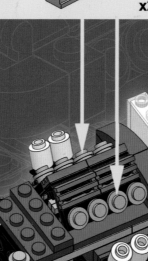

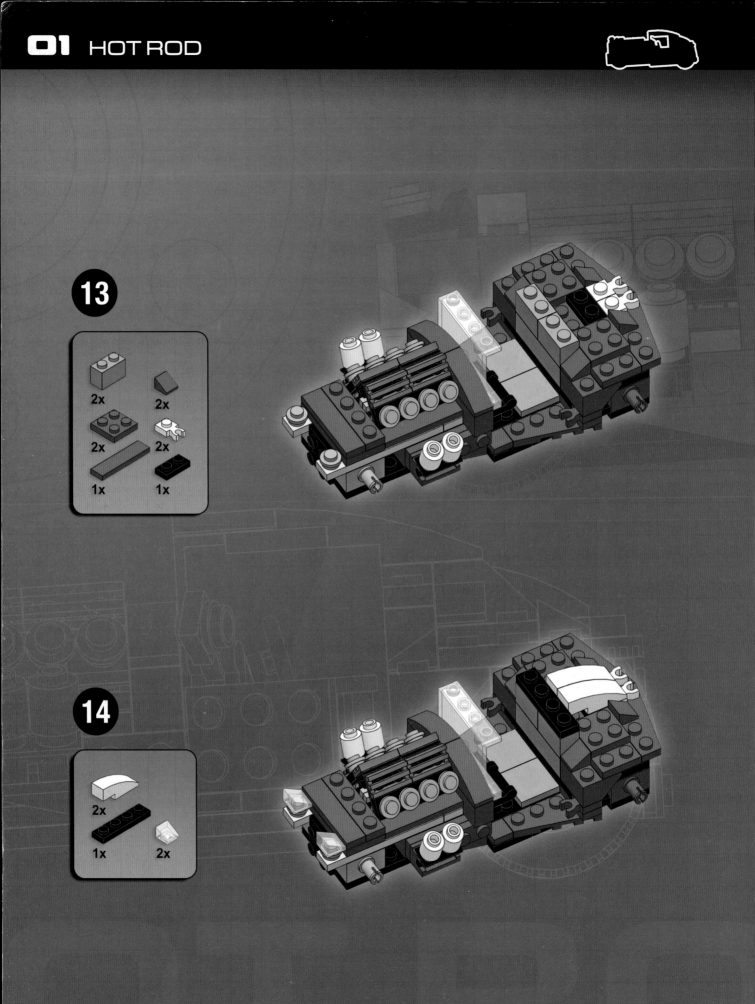

13

2x   2x

2x   2x

1x   1x

14

2x

1x   2x

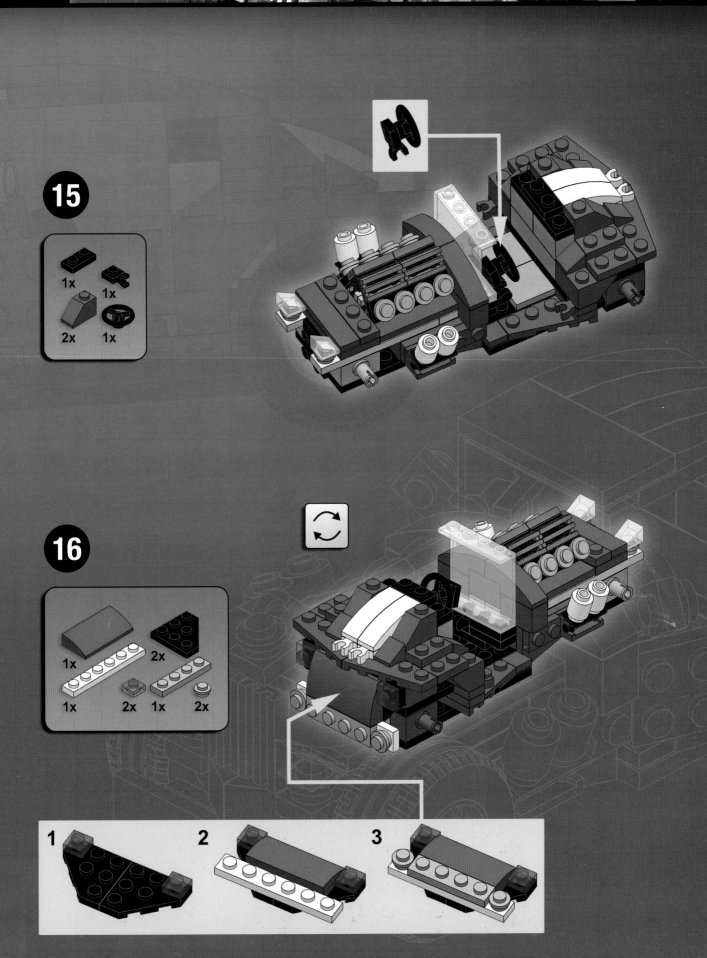

15

1x
1x
2x
1x

16

1x 2x
1x 2x 1x 2x

1 2 3

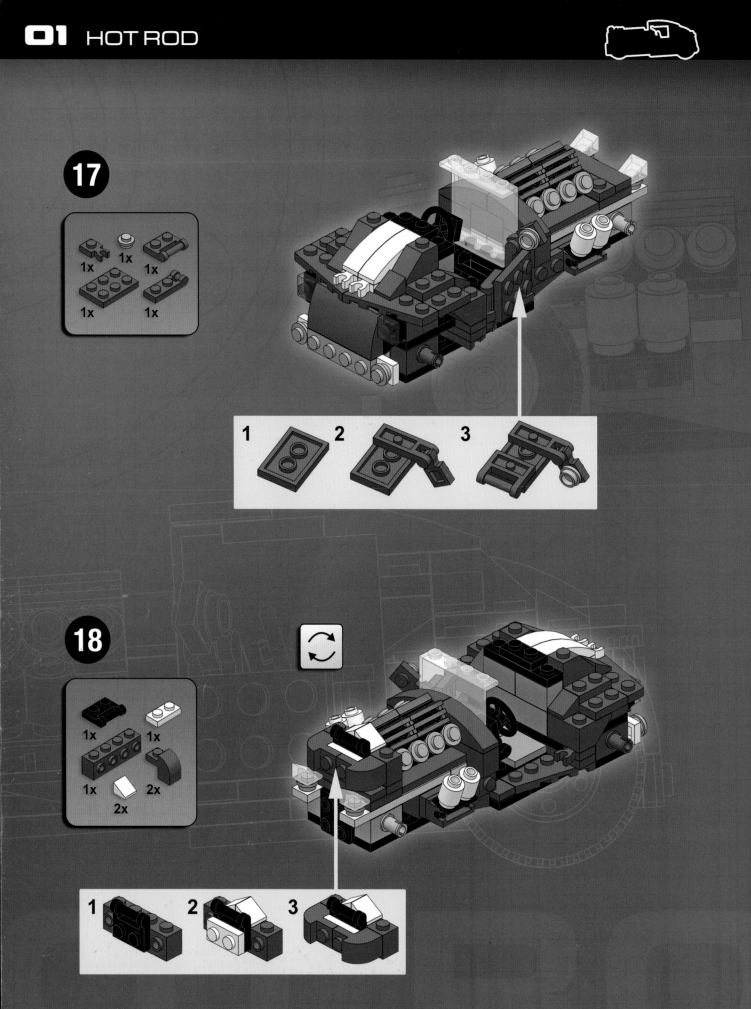

17

1x 1x 1x
1x 1x

1 2 3

18

1x 1x
1x 2x
2x

1 2 3

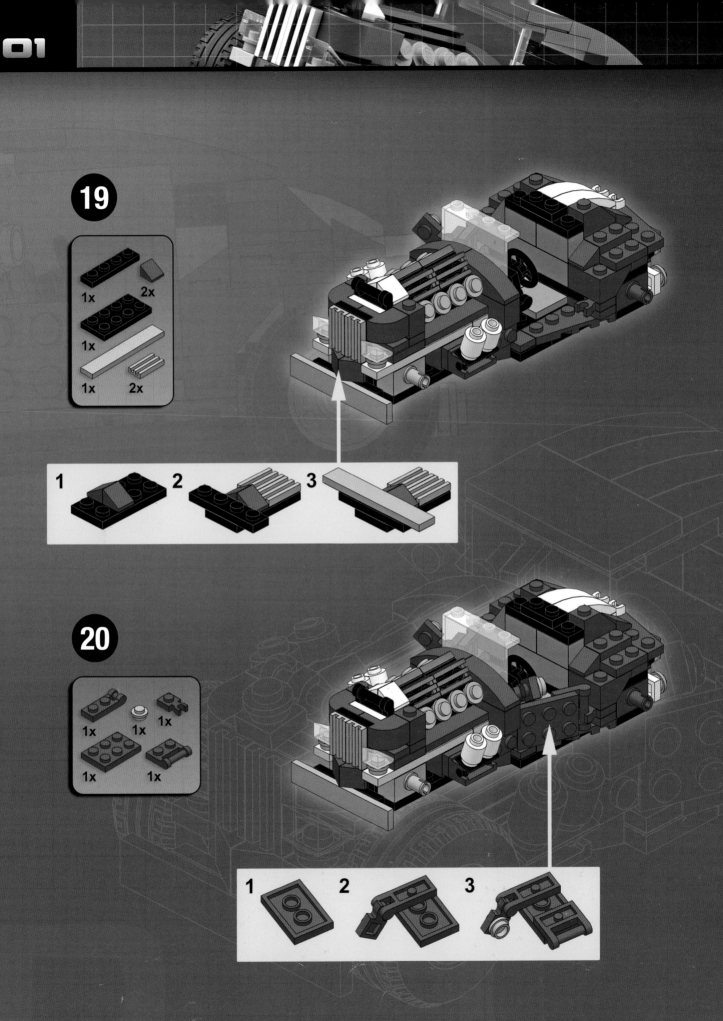

19

1x 2x
1x
1x 2x

1 2 3

20

1x 1x 1x
1x 1x

1 2 3

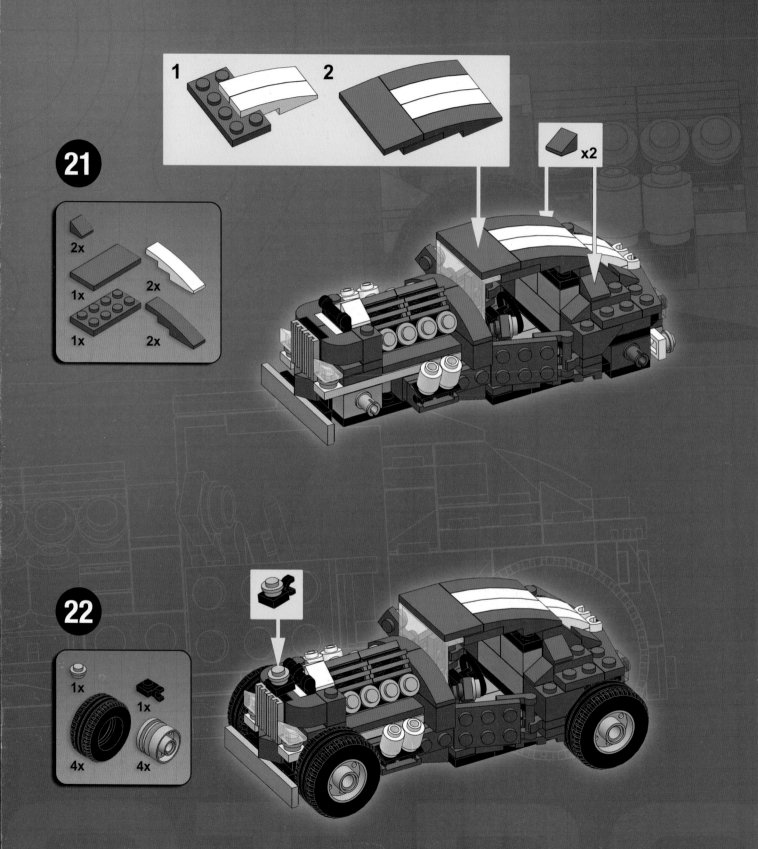

GRAN TURISMO

Design notes: low chassis, aerodynamic shape, sophisticated lines, racing stripes, spoiler

Technical specifications:

Dimensions (l × w × h):	20 × 9 × 7 studs
Wheelbase:	12 studs
Axle width front/rear:	8/8 studs

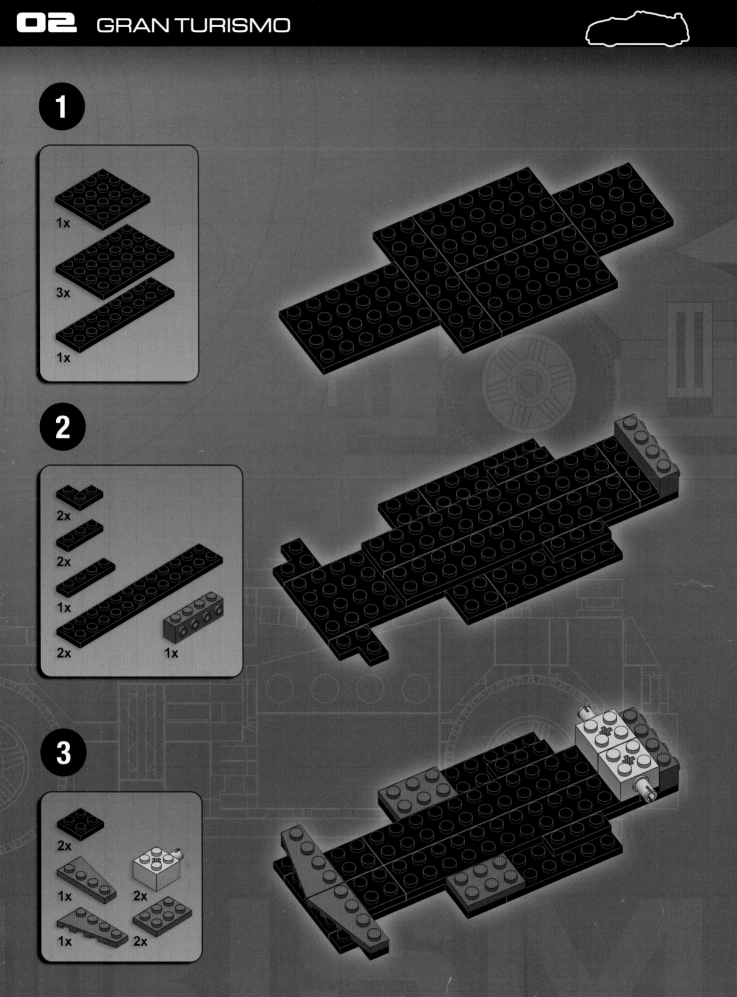

1

1x

3x

1x

2

2x

2x

1x

2x

1x

3

2x

1x

2x

1x

2x

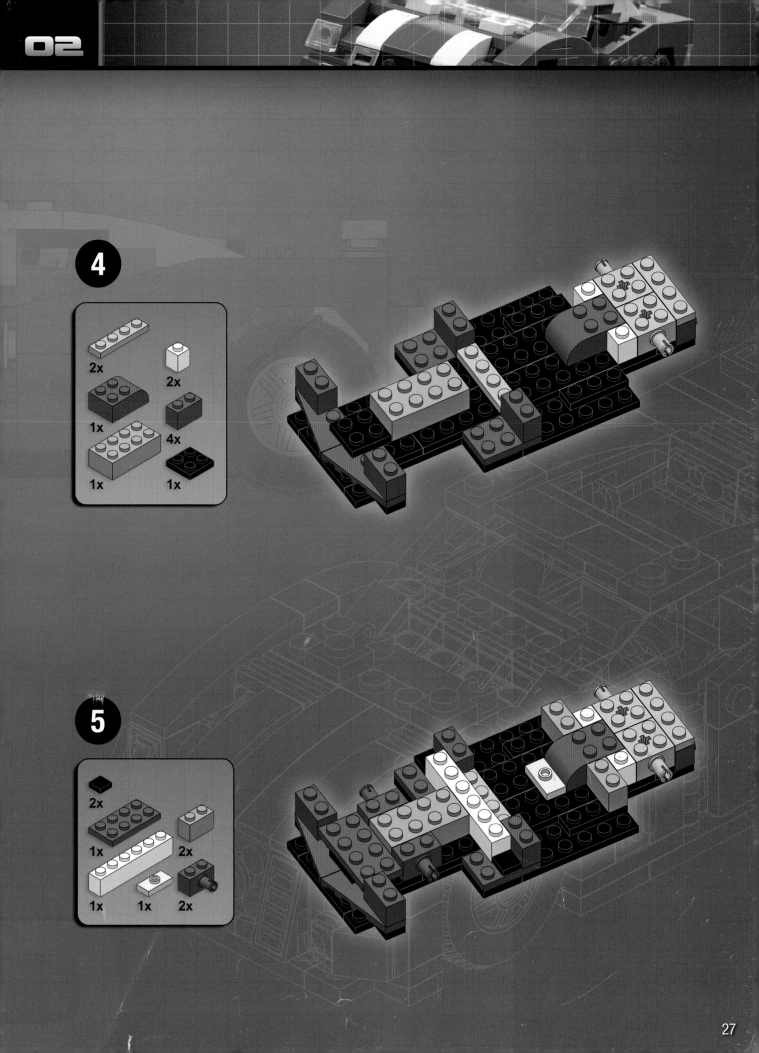

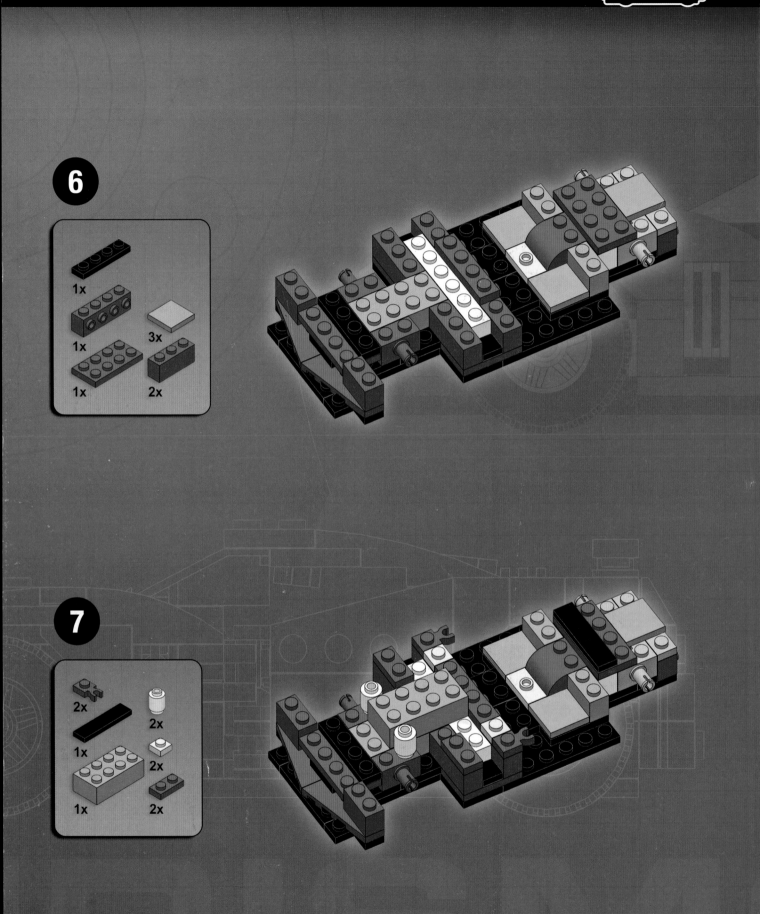

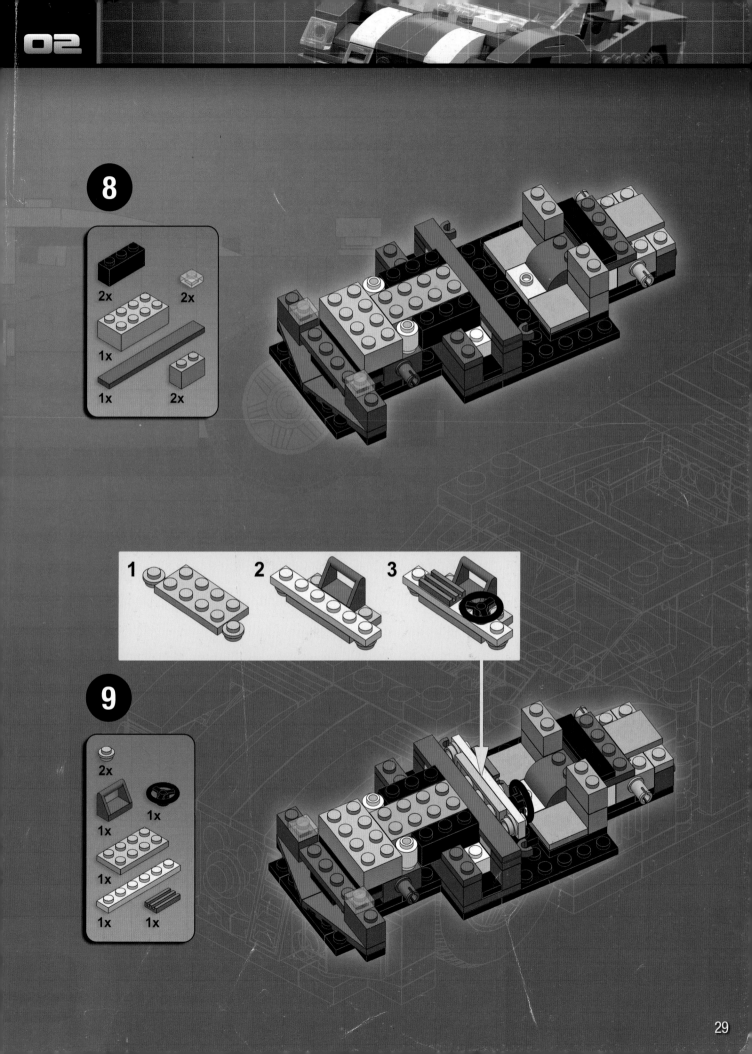

8

2x 2x
1x
1x 2x

1 2 3

9

2x
1x
1x
1x
1x 1x

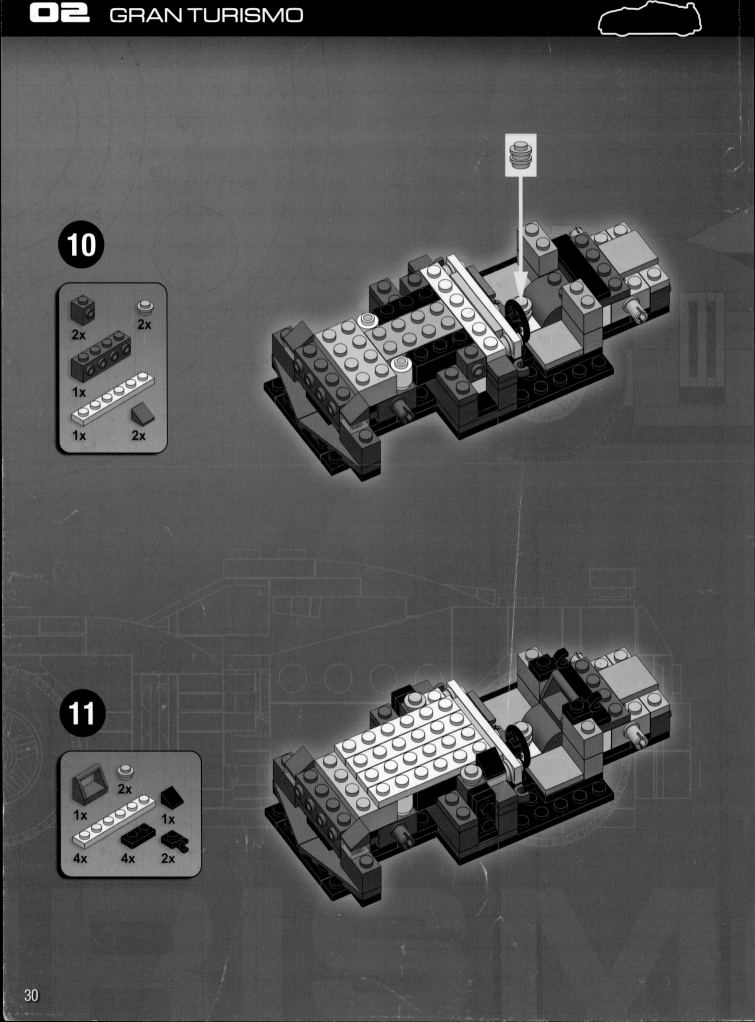

10

2x   2x
1x
1x   2x

11

1x   2x
      1x
4x   4x   2x

12

1x

1x

1x

1x

2x

1x

4x

2x

13

2x

1x

1x

2x

2x

14

2x **2x**
2x **2x**

15

2x

2x **2x**

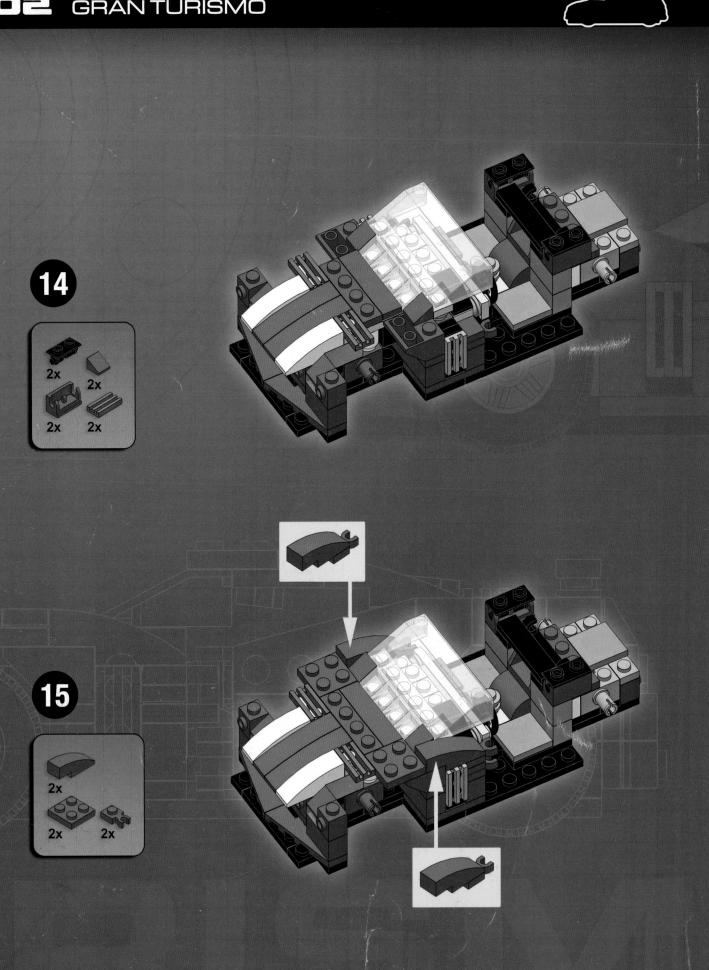

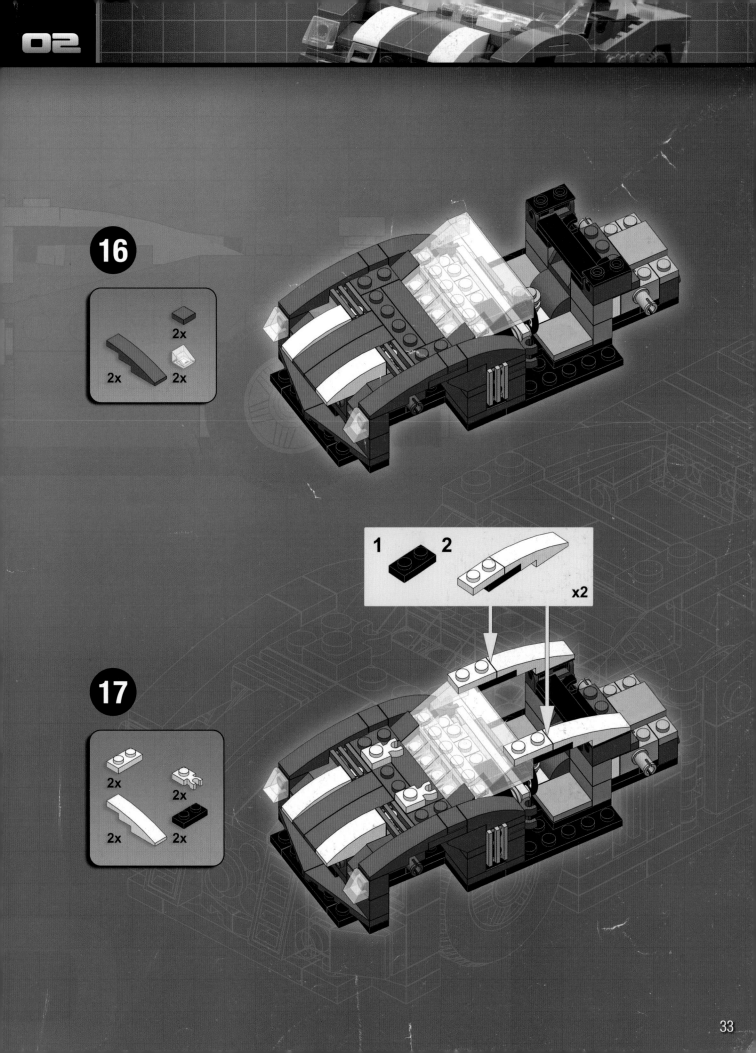

16

2x
2x
2x
2x

1   2   x2

17

2x
2x
2x
2x

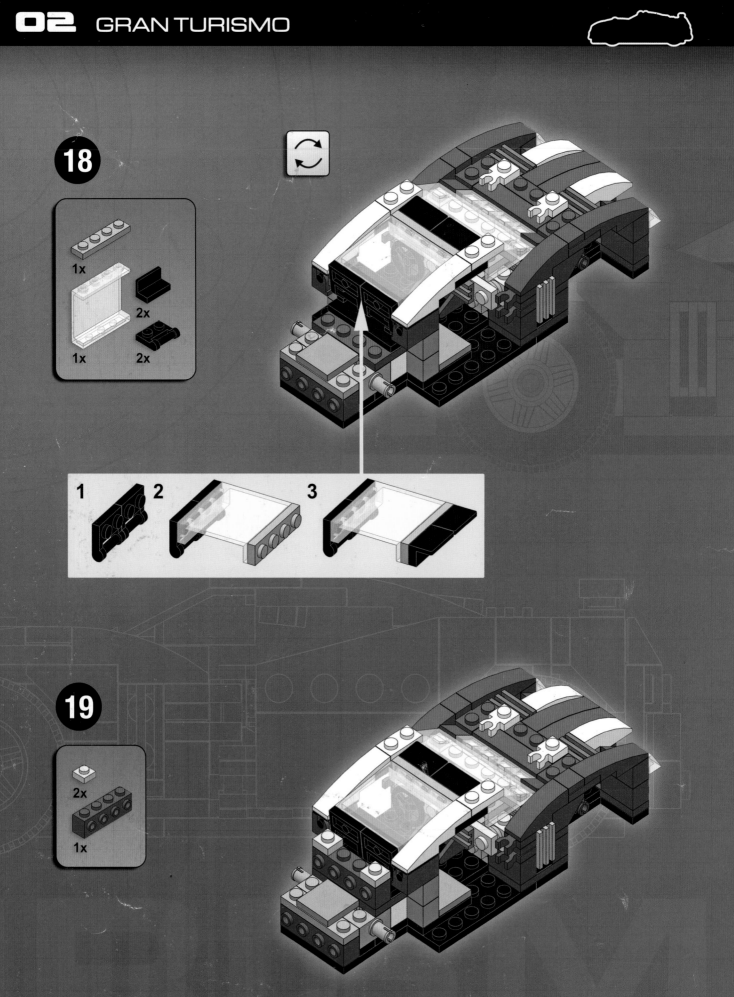

18

1x
2x
1x
2x

1 2 3

19

2x
1x

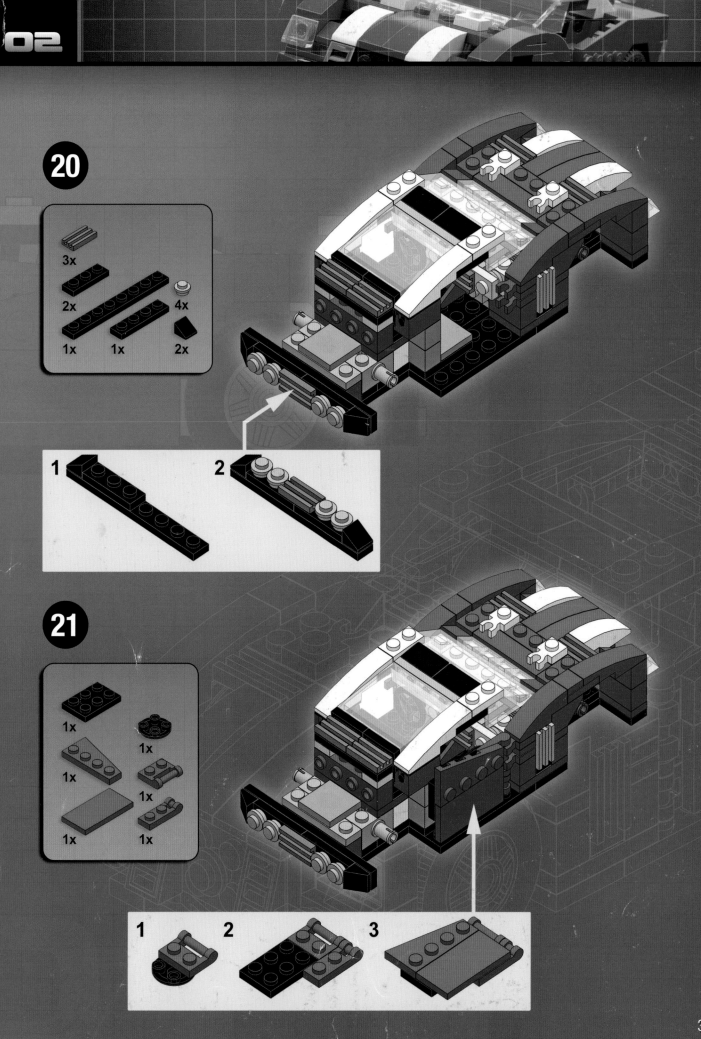

20

3x
2x
4x
1x
1x
2x

1
2

21

1x
1x
1x
1x
1x
1x

1
2
3

22

1

2x
1x   1x

2

2x
2x   2x

3

2x
2x
1x   2x

4

2x   3x
2x   2x

5

2x
1x   2x

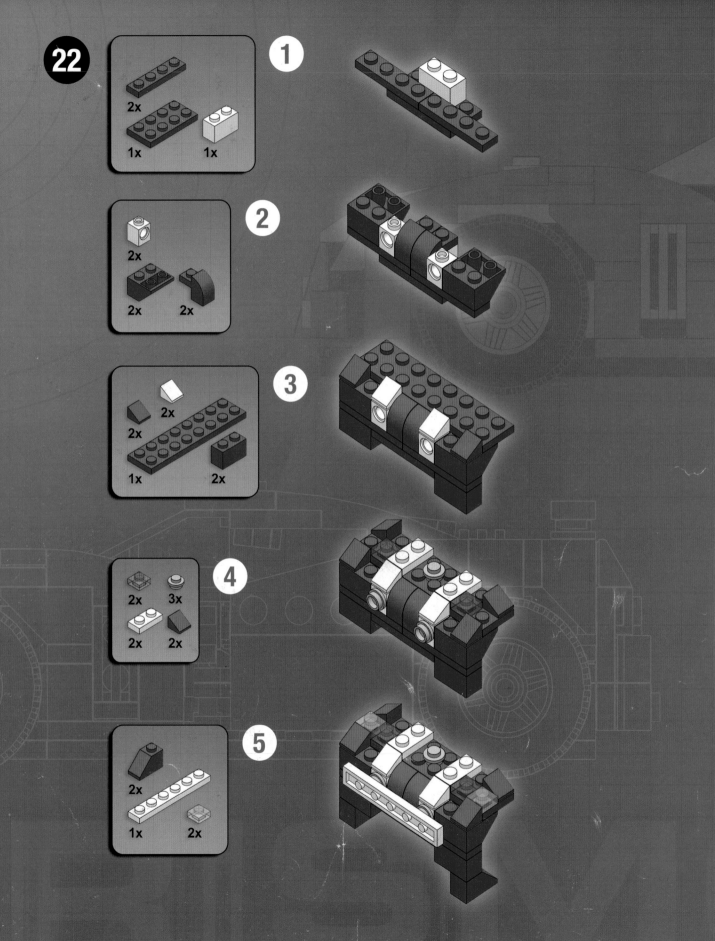

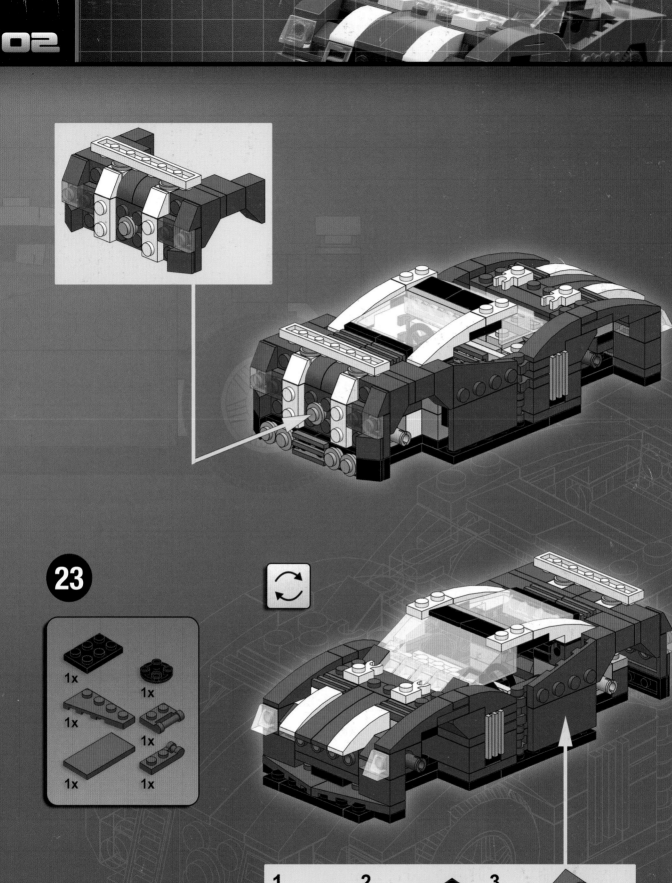

23

1x
1x
1x
1x
1x
1x

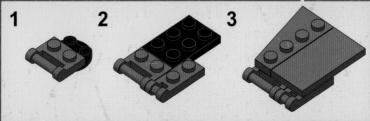

1   2   3

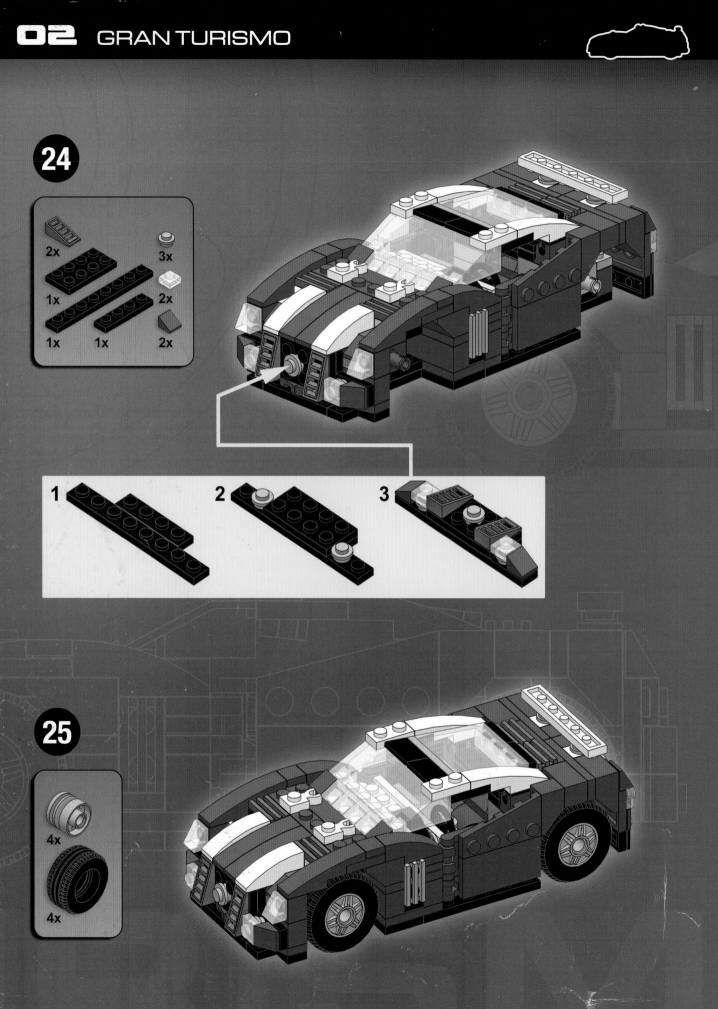

24

2x
3x
1x
2x
1x 1x 2x

1
2
3

25

4x
4x

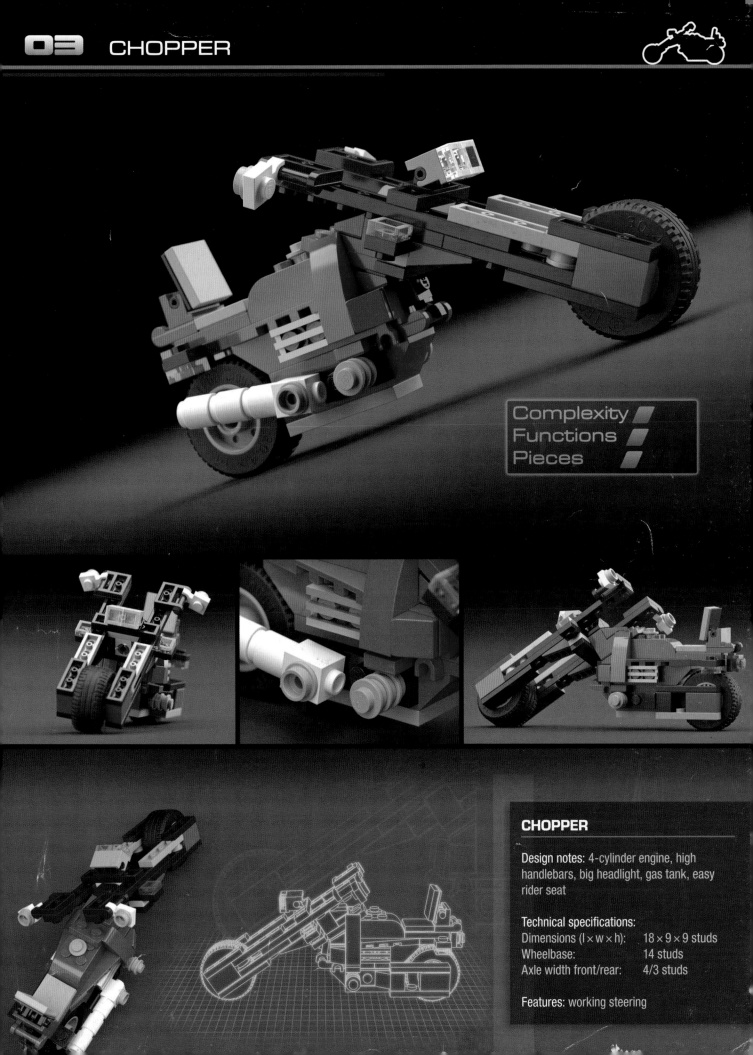

Complexity
Functions
Pieces

CHOPPER

Design notes: 4-cylinder engine, high handlebars, big headlight, gas tank, easy rider seat

Technical specifications:
Dimensions (l × w × h):	18 × 9 × 9 studs
Wheelbase:	14 studs
Axle width front/rear:	4/3 studs

Features: working steering

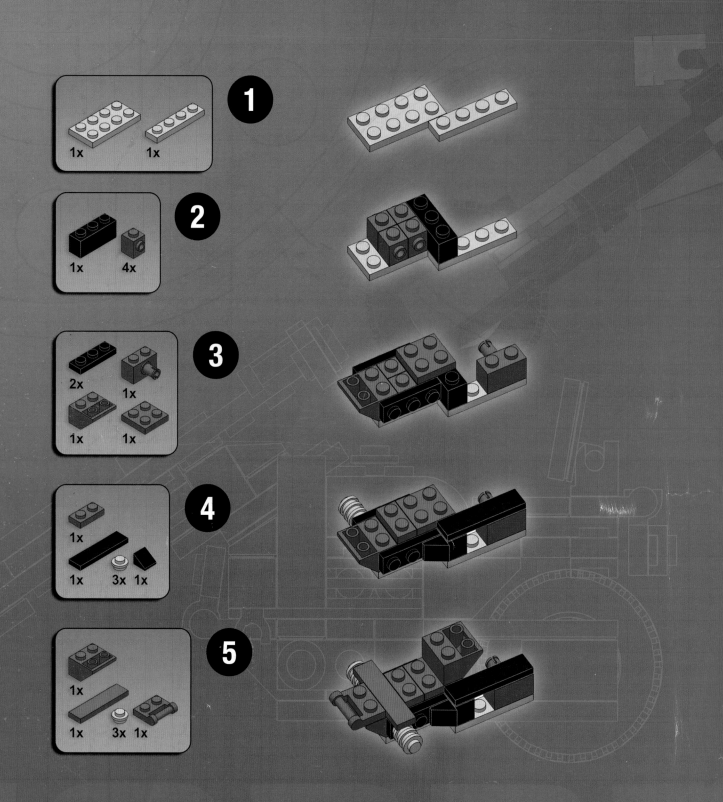

6

2x 4x

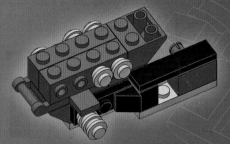

7

1x 2x
1x 2x

8

1x
1x 2x

9

1x 2x 1x

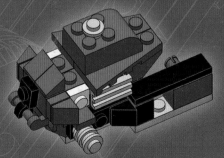

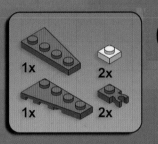

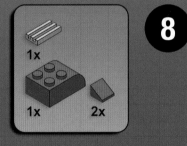

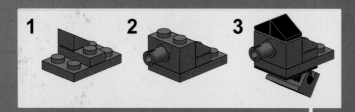

10

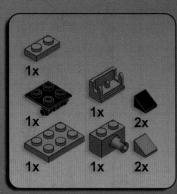

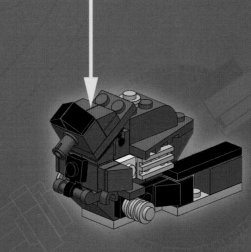

11

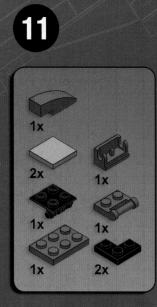

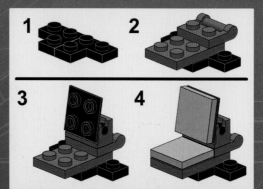

12

1

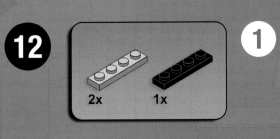

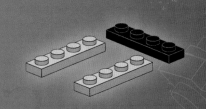

2

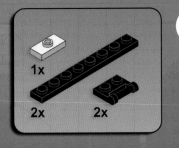

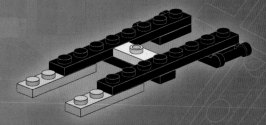

3

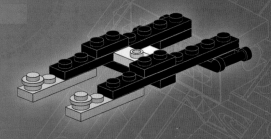

4

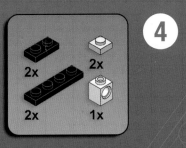

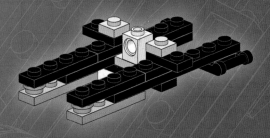

5

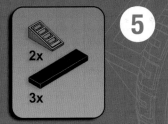

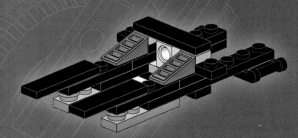

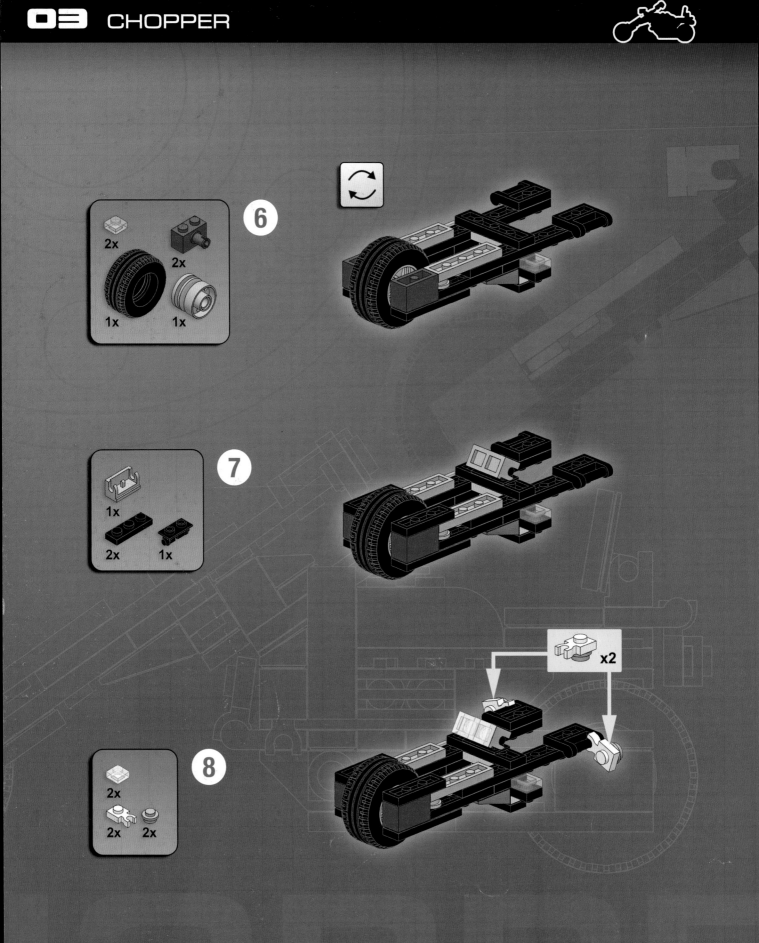

6

2x
2x
1x
1x

7

1x
2x
1x

x2

8

2x
2x   2x

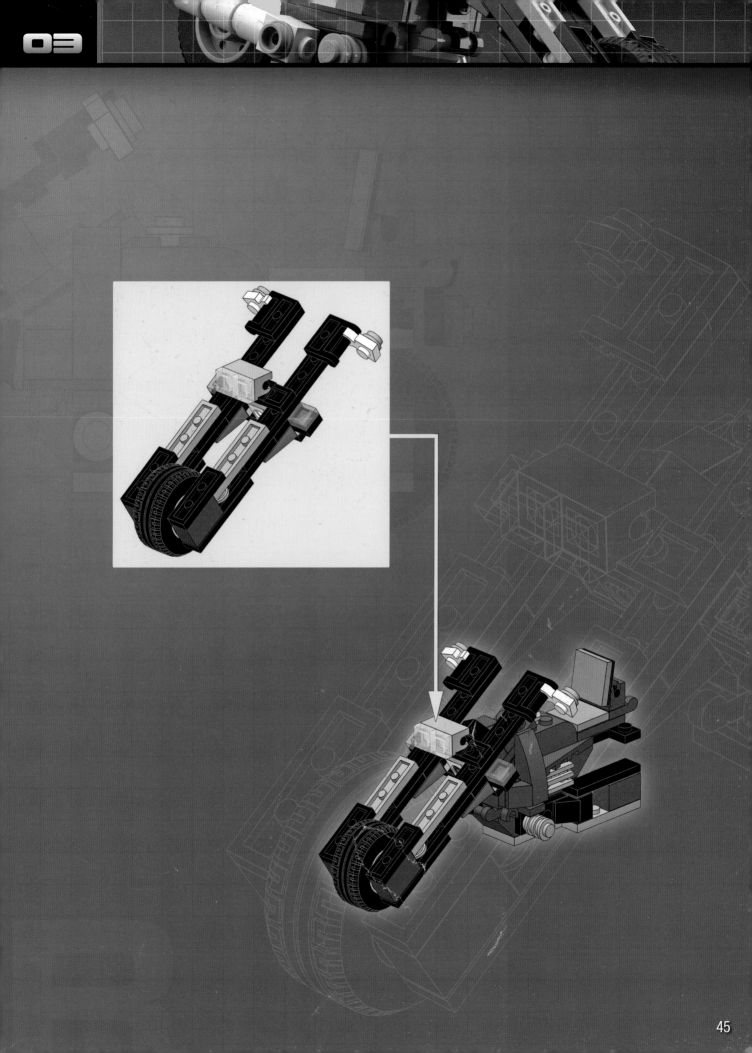

13

1x
1x
1x
1x
1x
1x

14

2x
1x
1x
3x

1   2

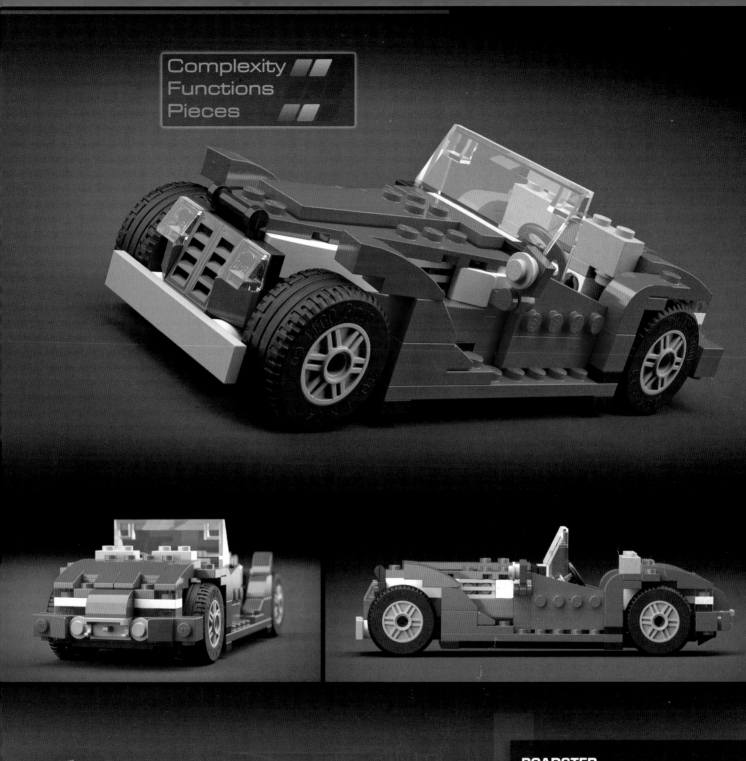

Complexity ▰▰
Functions
Pieces ▰▰

ROADSTER

Design notes: dramatic curves; open top; long, tapered nose; classic sporty design; detailed interior

Technical specifications:

Dimensions (l × w × h):	21 × 9 × 7 studs
Wheelbase:	14 studs
Axle width front/rear:	8/8 studs

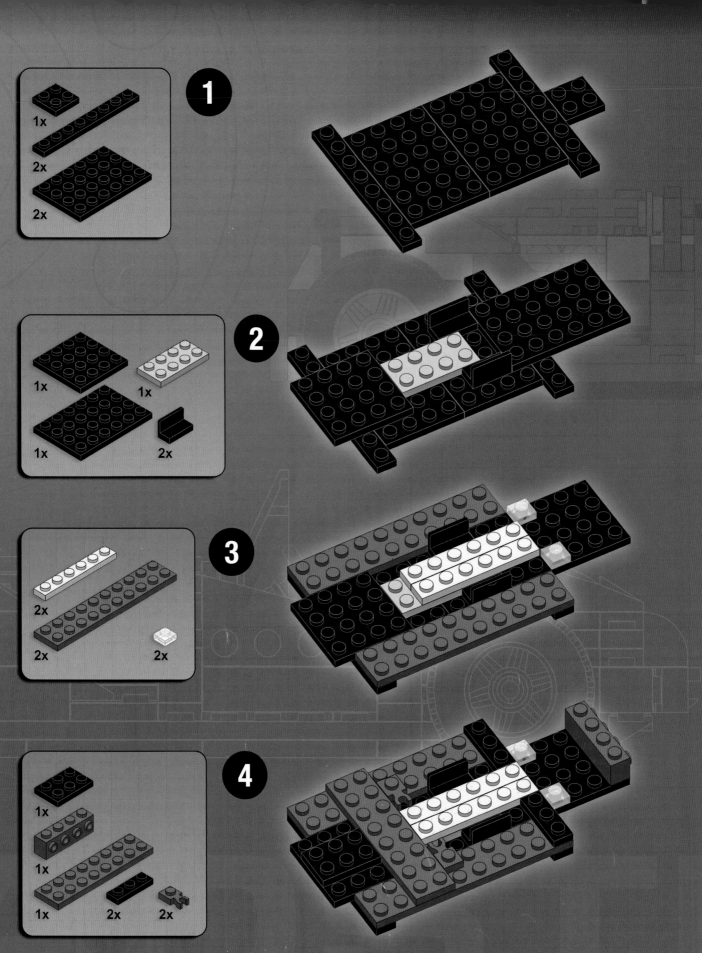

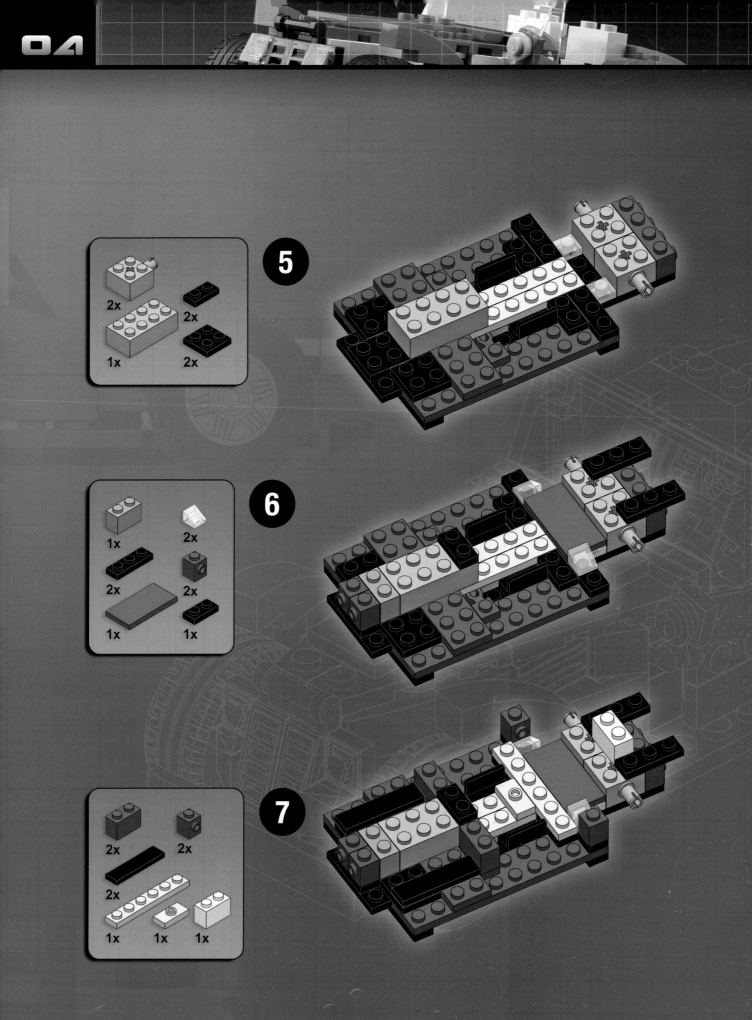

5

2x
2x
1x
2x

6

1x
2x
2x
2x
1x
1x

7

2x
2x
2x
1x
1x
1x

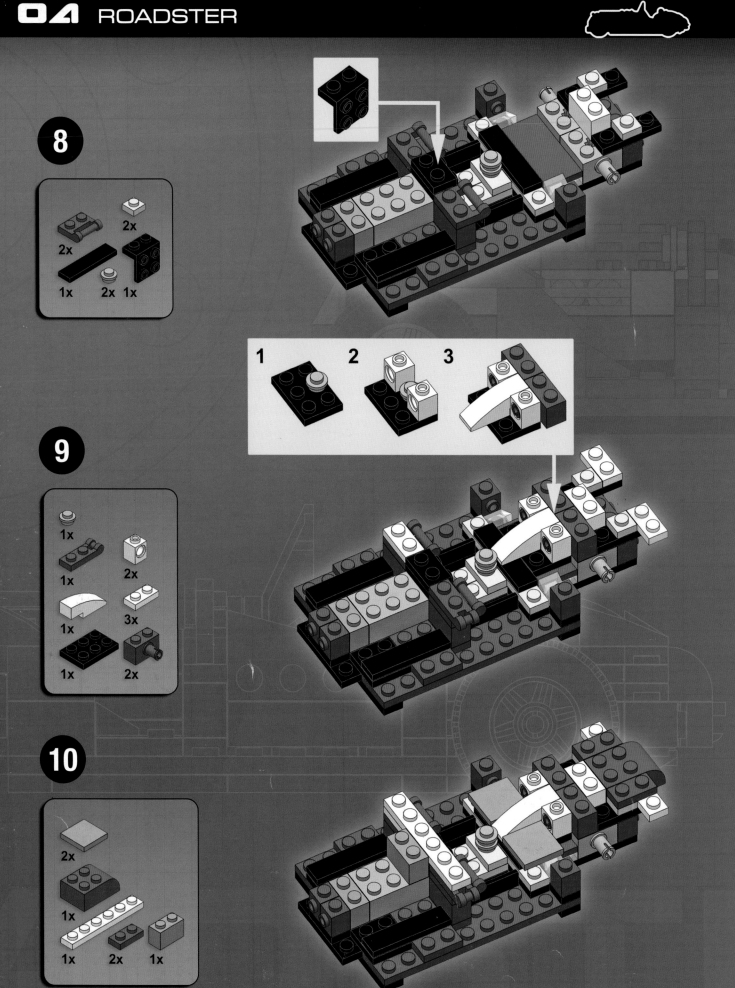

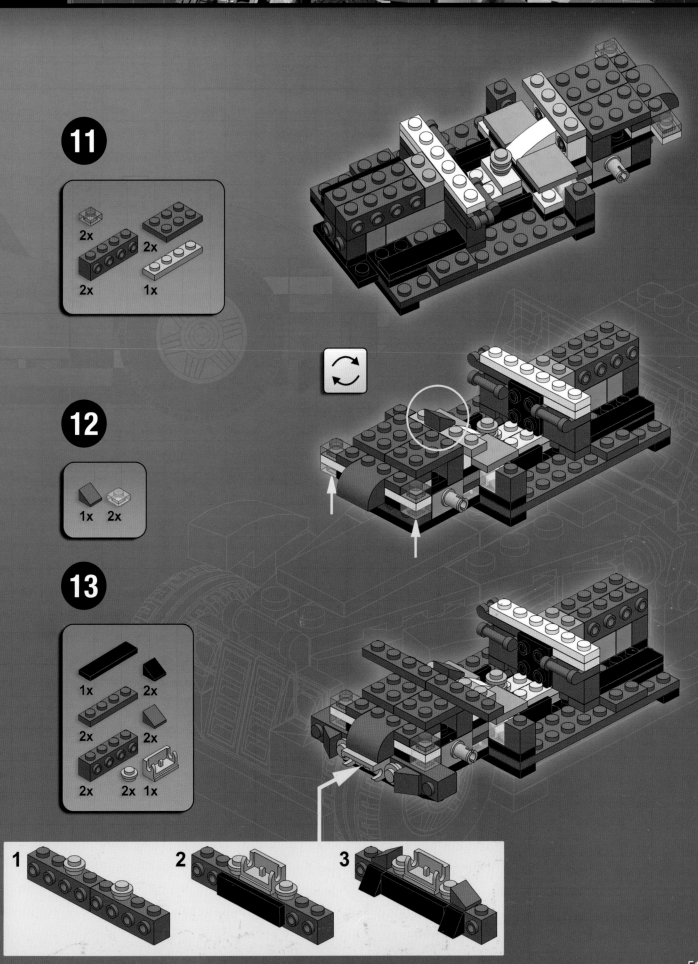

11

2x
2x
2x
1x

12

1x 2x

13

1x 2x
2x 2x
2x 2x 1x

1
2
3

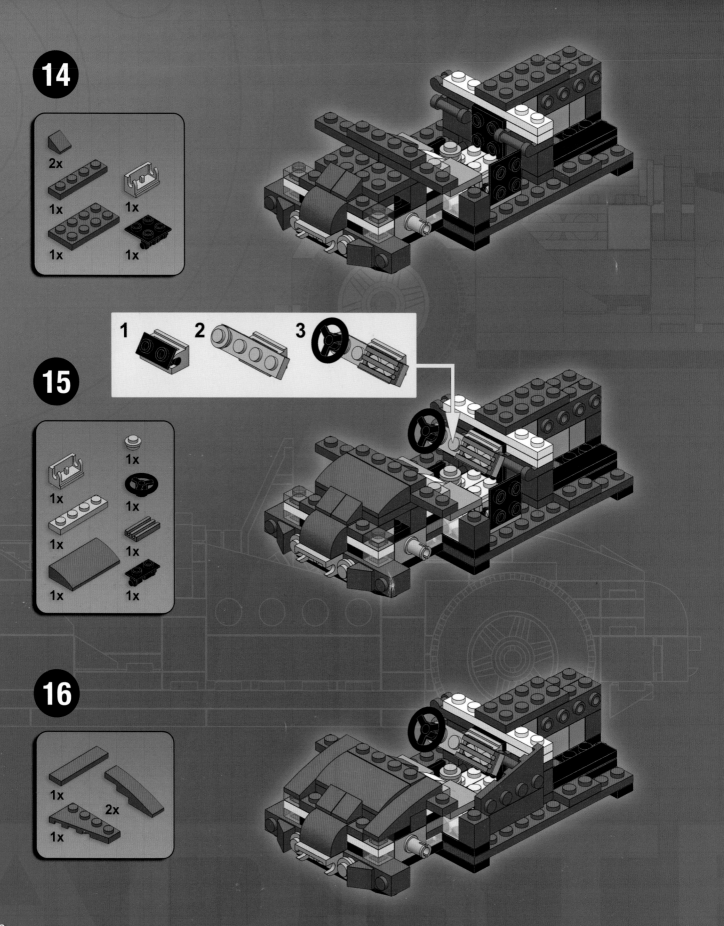

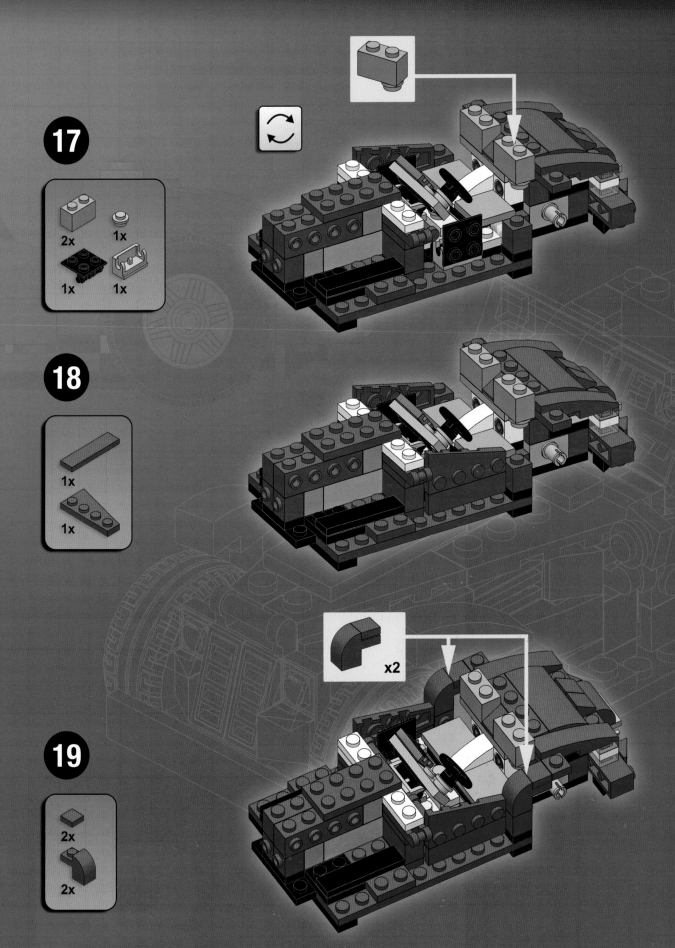

17

2x   1x
1x   1x

18

1x
1x

19

2x
2x

x2

20

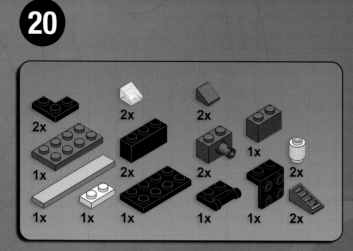

21

1x

1x   1x

22

3x

1x

1x   1x

1x   1x

1x   1x

1x   1x

1   **2**

3   **4**

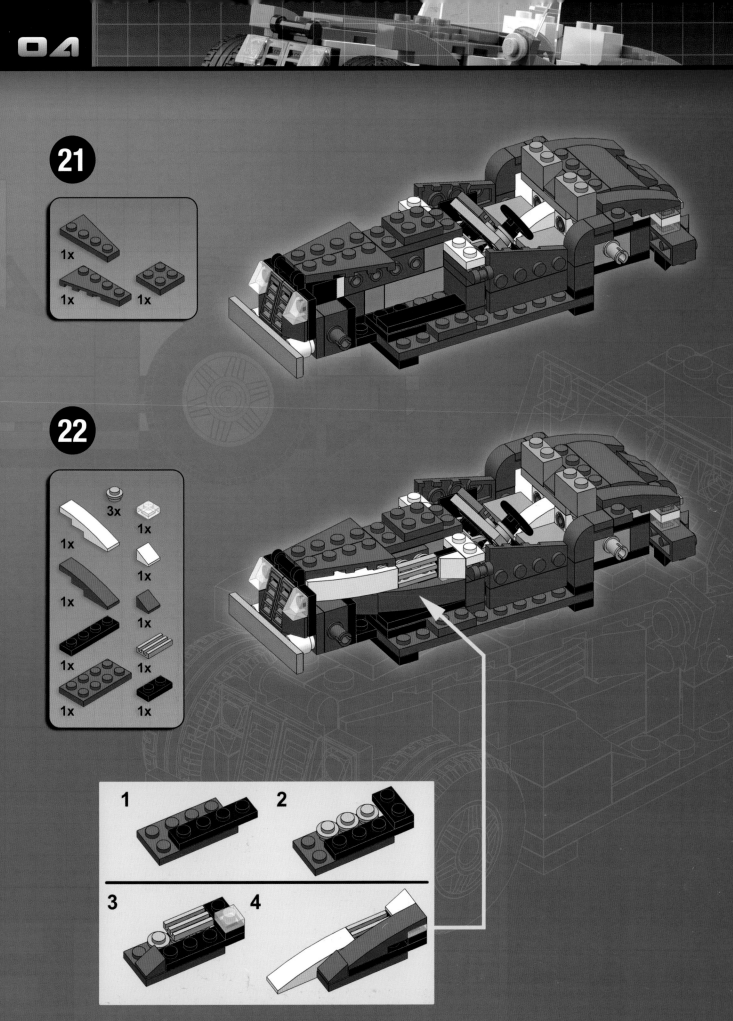

23

3x
1x
1x
1x
1x
1x
1x
1x
1x
1x

1
2
3
4

24

1x
1x
1x
1x

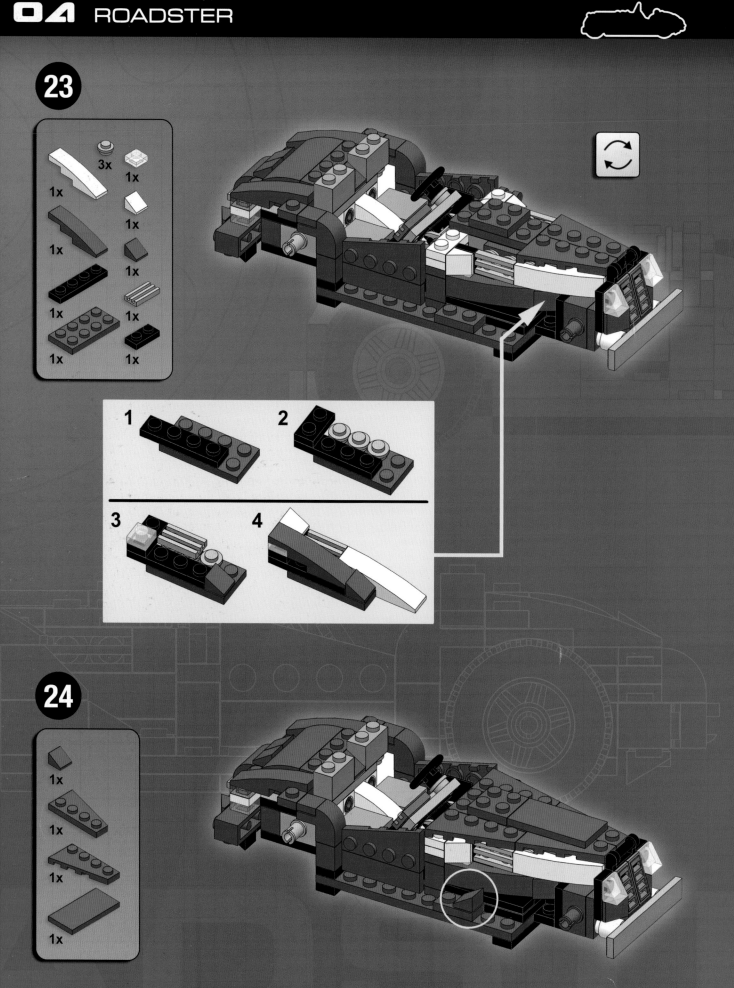

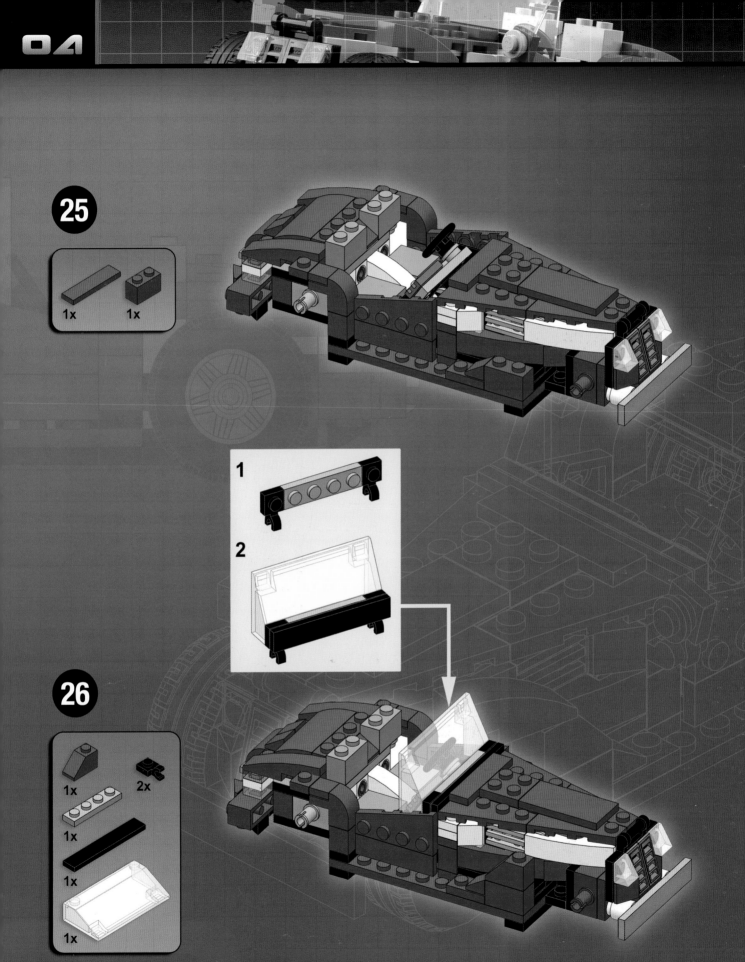

25

1x   1x

1

2

26

1x   2x

1x

1x

1x

27

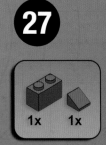

1x   1x

28

1x
1x   1x

29

4x

2x

4x

Complexity
Functions
Pieces

WRECKER

Design notes: long wheelbase, high clearance, flat bed, wide rear axle, massive grille, livery lines

Technical specifications:
Dimensions (l × w × h):   23 × 10 × 11 studs
Wheelbase: 14 studs
Axle width front/rear: 8/10 studs

Features: lifting crane

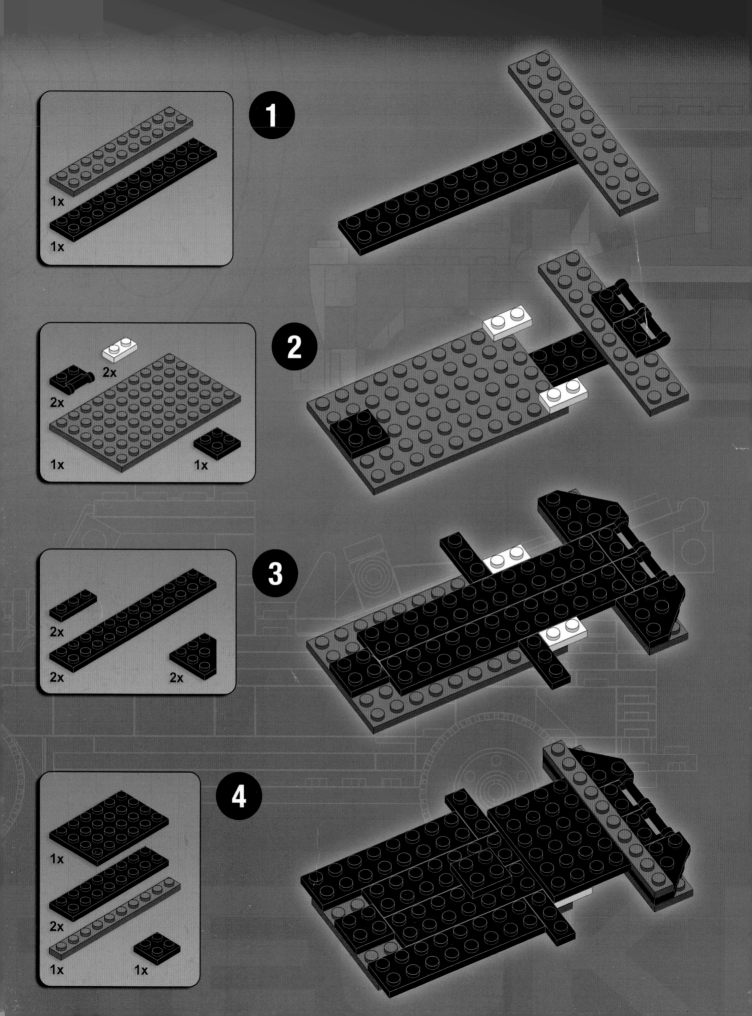

1

1x

1x

2

2x

2x

1x

1x

3

2x

2x

2x

4

1x

2x

1x

1x

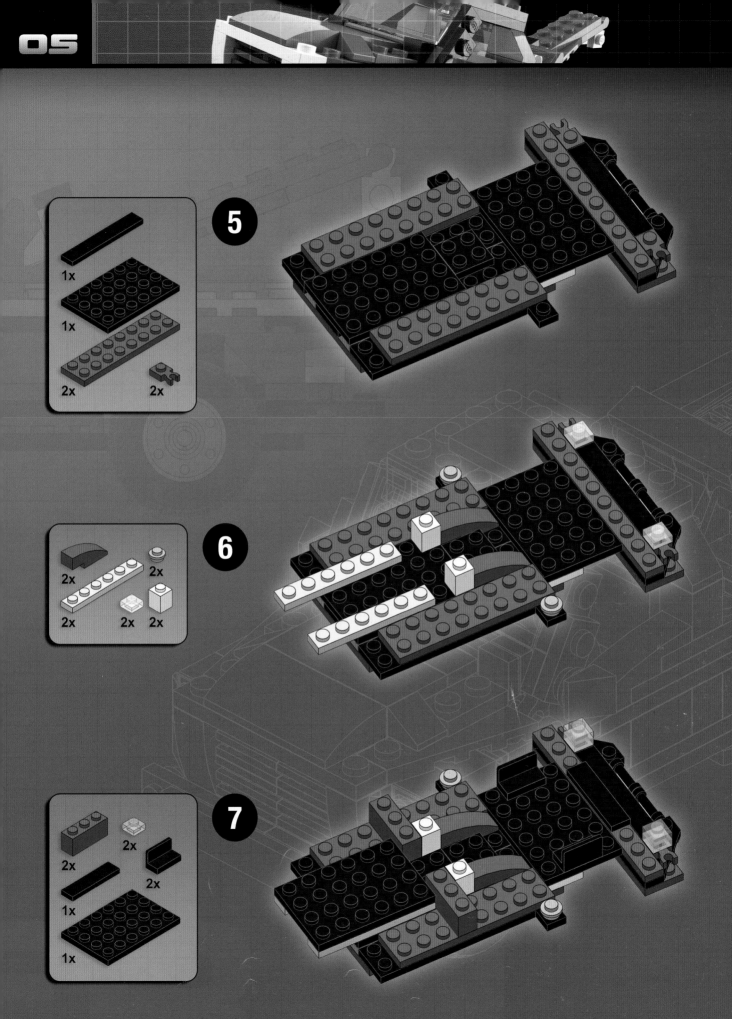

5

1x
1x
2x   2x

6

2x   2x
2x   2x   2x

7

2x
2x   2x
1x
1x

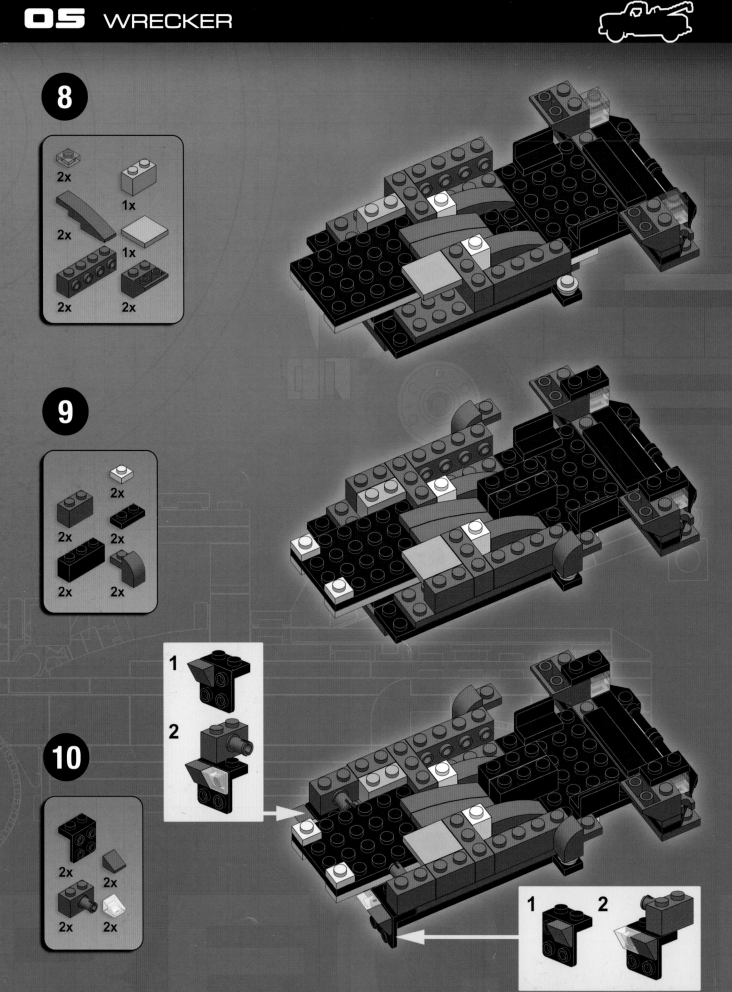

8

2x
1x
2x
1x
2x 2x

9

2x
2x
2x
2x
2x

10

1
2

2x
2x
2x
2x

1 2

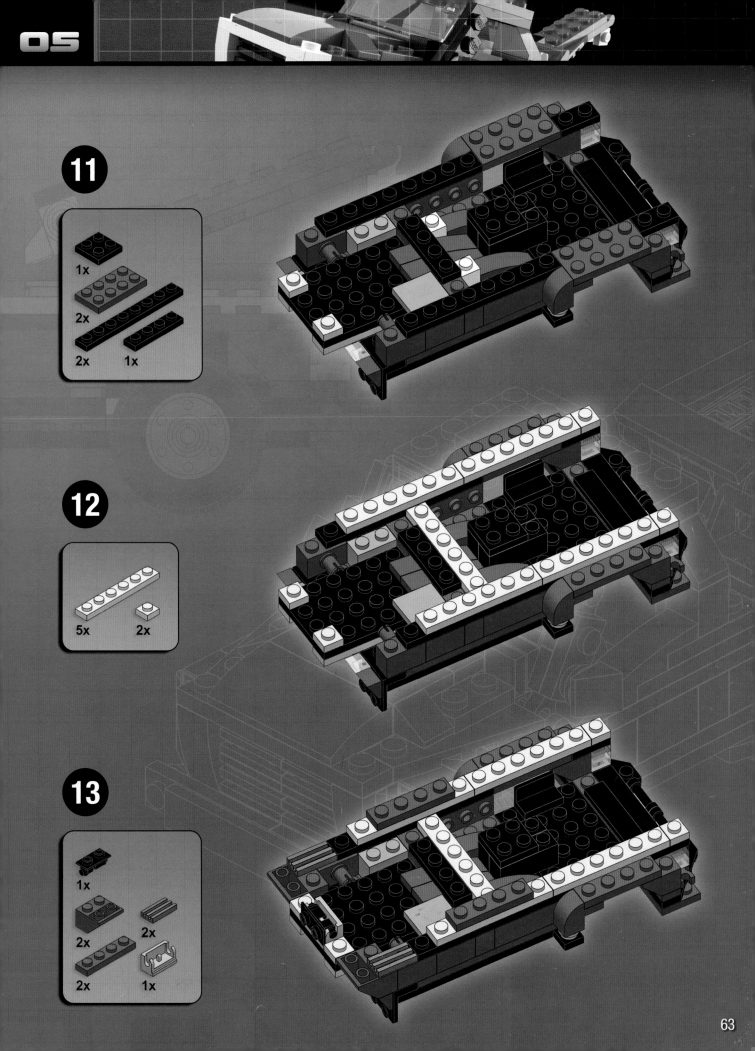

11

1x
2x
2x 1x

12

5x 2x

13

1x
2x 2x
2x 1x

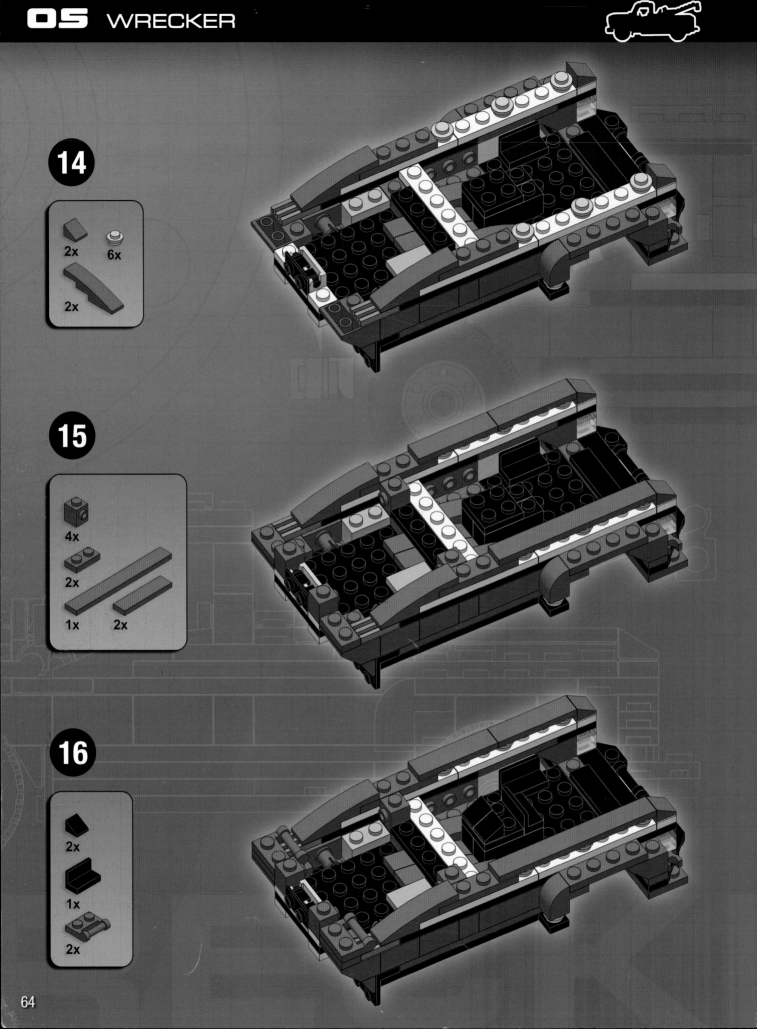

14

2x 6x

2x

15

4x

2x

1x 2x

16

2x

1x

2x

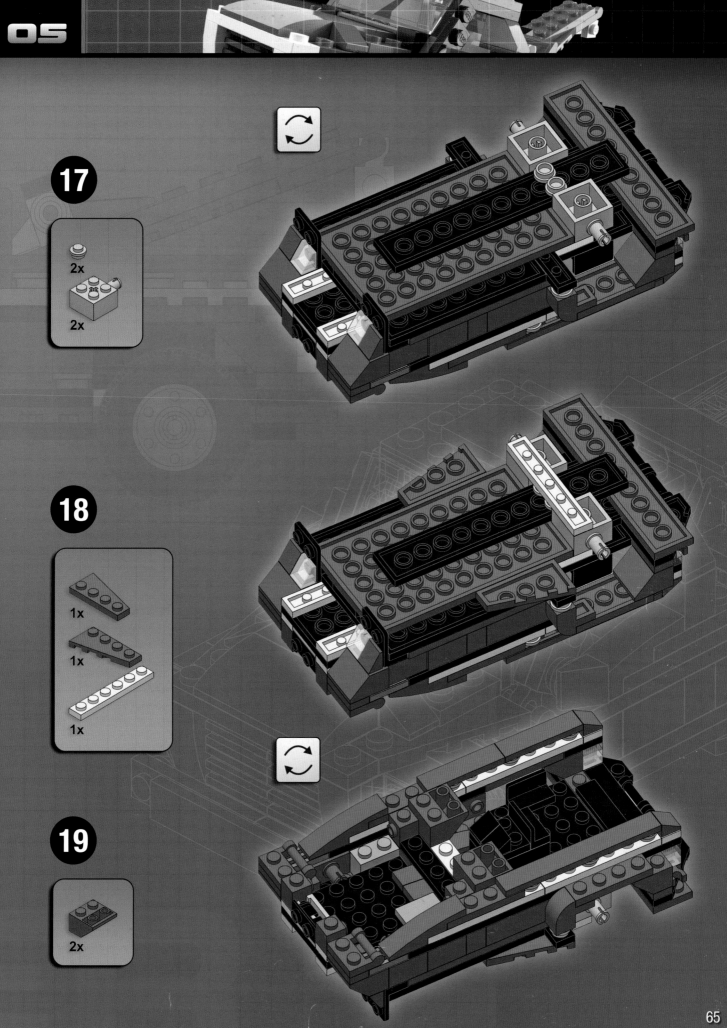

17

2x

2x

18

1x

1x

1x

19

2x

20

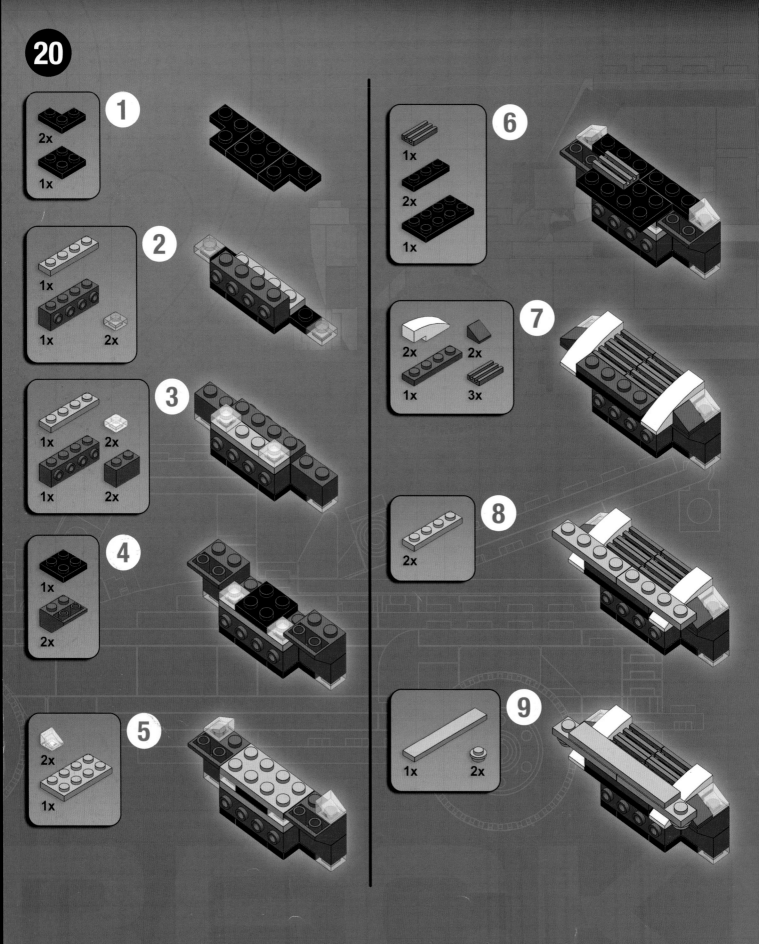

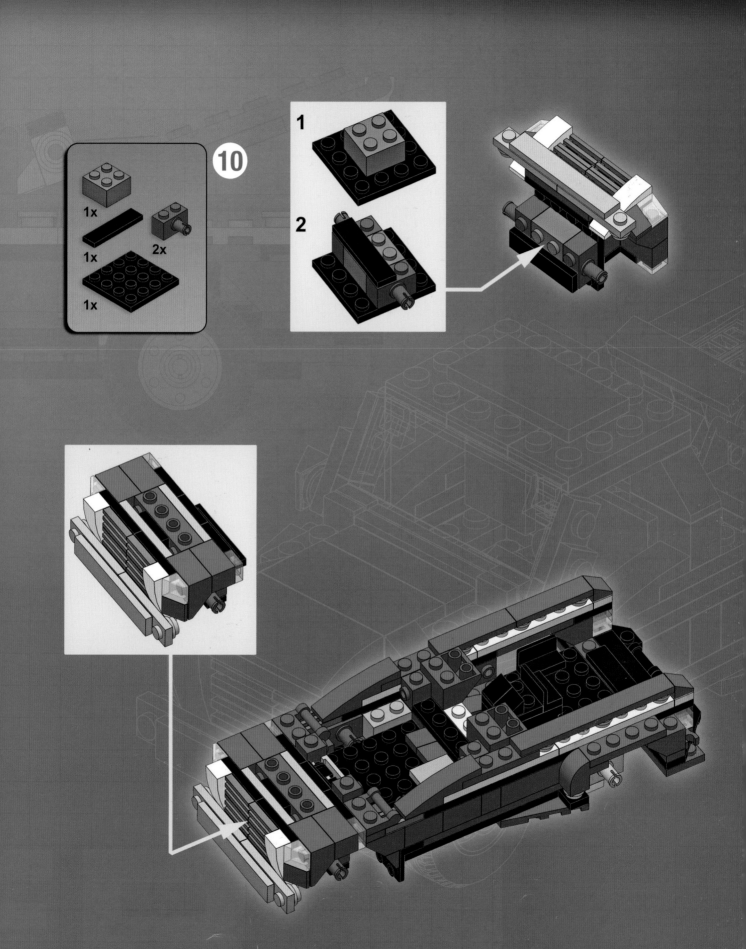

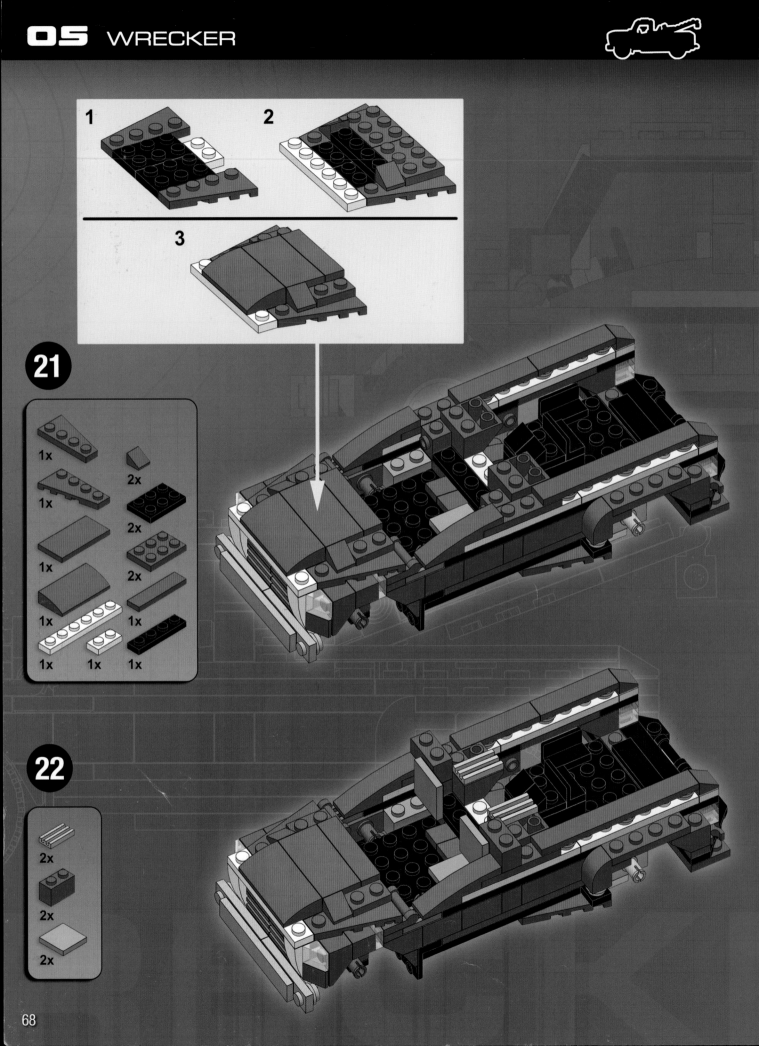

1

2

3

21

1x
2x
1x
1x
2x
1x
2x
1x
1x
1x
1x

22

2x
2x
2x

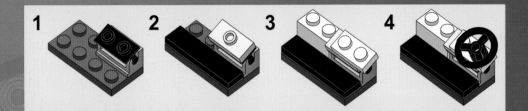

1 2 3 4

23

1x 1x
1x 1x
1x 1x
1x 1x

24

1x 2x
1x 2x

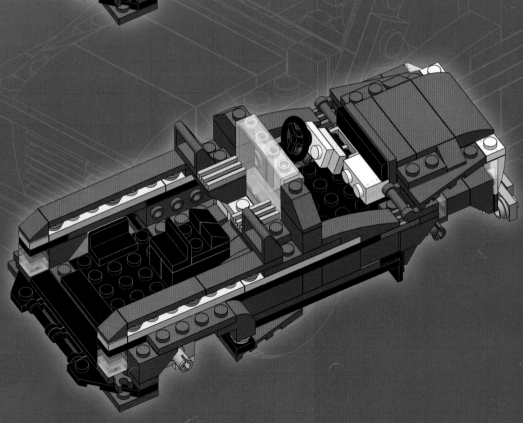

25

1x

1

2

1x 2x
1x 1x 1x

3

2x
2x

4

2x
2x

5

2x
1x

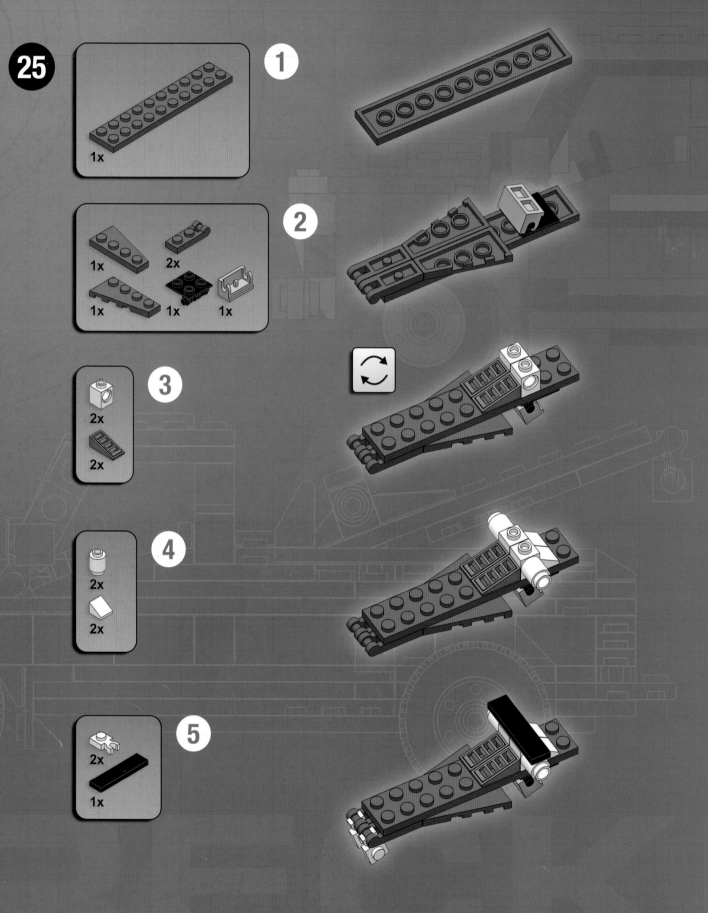

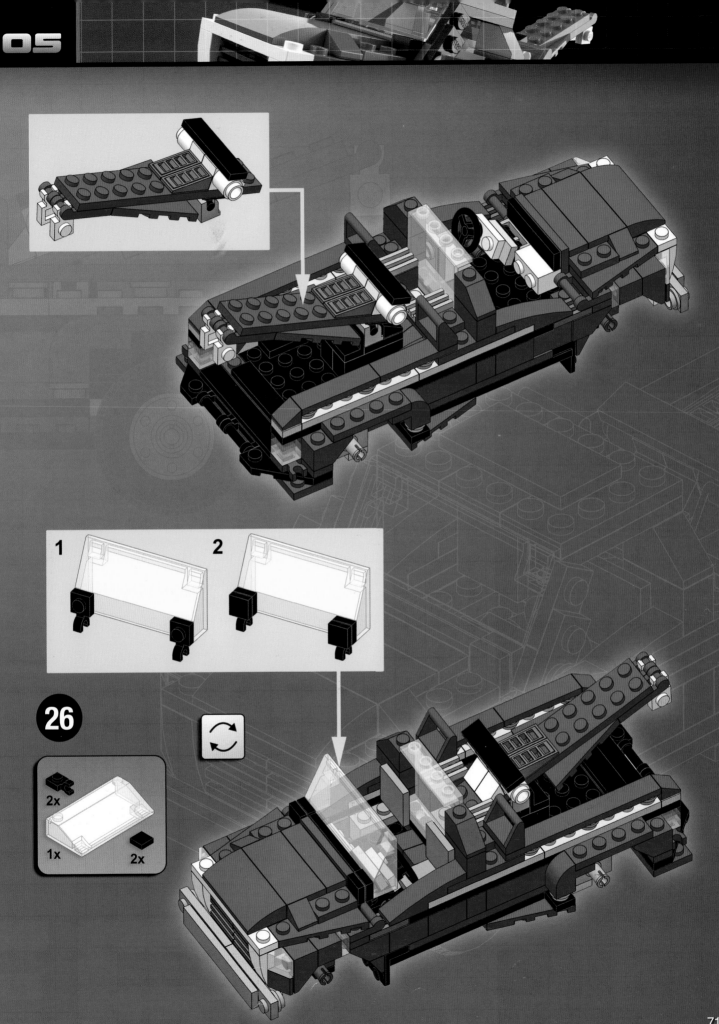

1
2

26

2x
1x
2x

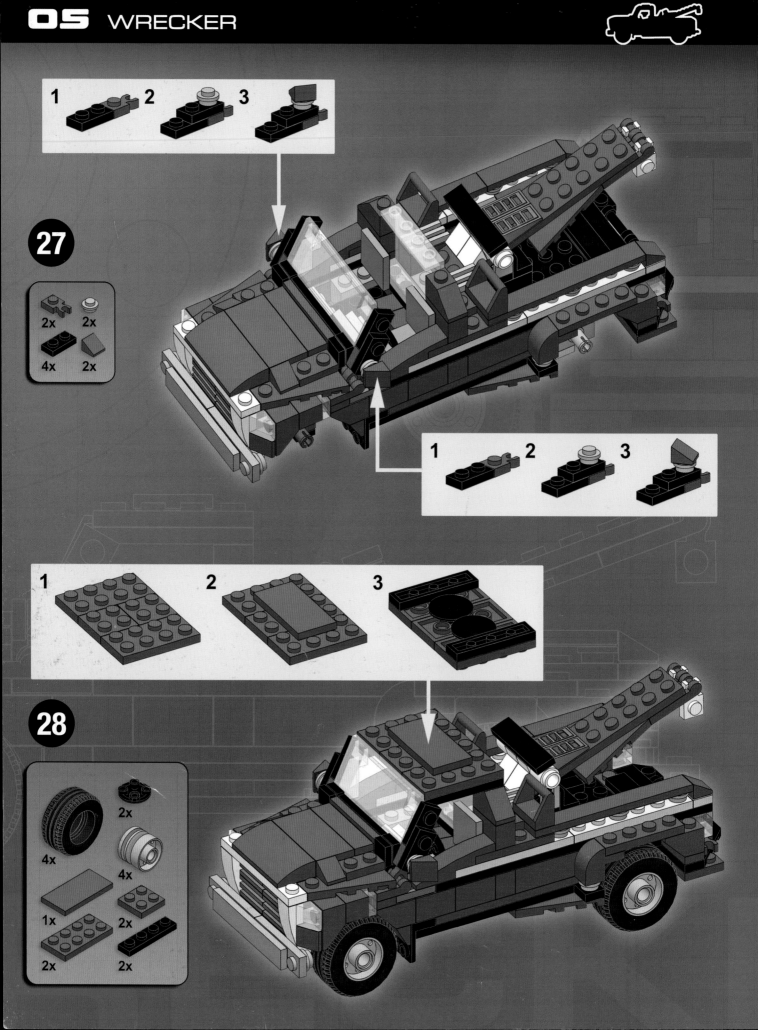

27

28

BUILDING TIPS

THREE IMPORTANT QUESTIONS

WHEN YOU DESIGN A MODEL OF A VEHICLE, START BY THINKING ABOUT ITS PURPOSE. IS IT A SPEED MACHINE, OR IS IT AN OFF-ROAD BEAST MEANT TO BE STABLE ON ROCKY GROUND?

TO PLAN THE STRUCTURE AND PROPORTIONS OF YOUR VEHICLE, CONSIDER THESE THREE IMPORTANT QUESTIONS:

WHAT AM I GOING TO BUILD?

1. WHERE ARE THE WHEELS?

HEAVY-DUTY VEHICLES NEED A LONG WHEELBASE AND HIGH CLEARANCE TO COPE WITH ROUGH TERRAIN AND HEFTY LOADS.

LONG AND HIGH

SPEEDSTERS WILL BE SLUNG CLOSE TO THE GROUND TO INCREASE STABILITY.

SHORT AND LOW

RACE CARS COMBINE THE BEST OF BOTH WORLDS IN ORDER TO ACHIEVE MAXIMUM PERFORMANCE.

VERY LONG AND VERY LOW

2. WHERE IS THE ENGINE?

IN MOST VEHICLES, THE ENGINE IS BETWEEN THE FRONT WHEELS.

BUT RACE CARS OFTEN HAVE AN ENGINE BETWEEN THE FRONT AND REAR AXLES. HAVING THE WEIGHT OF THE ENGINE IN THE CENTER OF THE CAR PROVIDES GREATER BALANCE AND HANDLING, SO DRIVERS CAN TAKE CURVES AT EXTREME SPEEDS.

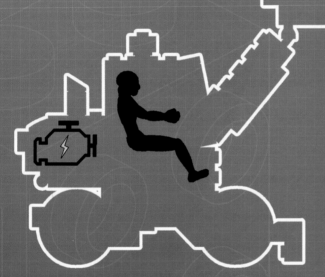

FOR CONSTRUCTION VEHICLES THAT NEED TO LIFT HEAVY LOADS, THE ENGINE IS OFTEN MOUNTED IN THE REAR, WHERE IT ACTS AS A COUNTERWEIGHT.

3. WHERE IS THE DRIVER SEATED?

THE DRIVER SITS BEHIND THE ENGINE IN MOST STANDARD CARS, BUT HE OR SHE MIGHT SIT IN FRONT OF THE ENGINE IN A CONSTRUCTION VEHICLE OR A TRUE RACING CAR.

IN "CAB-OVER" TRUCKS AND BUSES, THE DRIVER IS SEATED ABOVE THE ENGINE.

CONSIDER THESE QUESTIONS WHEN YOU DESIGN YOUR MODELS, AND YOU'LL BE ABLE TO BUILD YOUR VERY OWN AMAZING VEHICLES IN NO TIME.

PUT YOUR BEST FACE FORWARD

ONCE YOU HAVE A GOOD BASE FOR YOUR VEHICLE, IT'S TIME TO DRESS IT UP WITH DETAILS. SMALL TOUCHES CAN GIVE A VEHICLE UNIQUE CHARACTER AND EXTRA REALISM. THE FRONT OF A CAR IS VERY IMPORTANT—IT'S SOMETHING LIKE A PERSON'S FACE! THINK ABOUT DETAILS—LIKE HEADLIGHTS, GRILLES, COOLING VENTS FOR THE ENGINE, AND REARVIEW MIRRORS—THAT CAN MAKE THE DESIGN REALLY POP. (JUST DON'T FORGET TO ADD SOME DETAIL TO THE SIDES AND REAR AS WELL.)

WOW! WHAT A BUNCH OF PRETTY FACES!

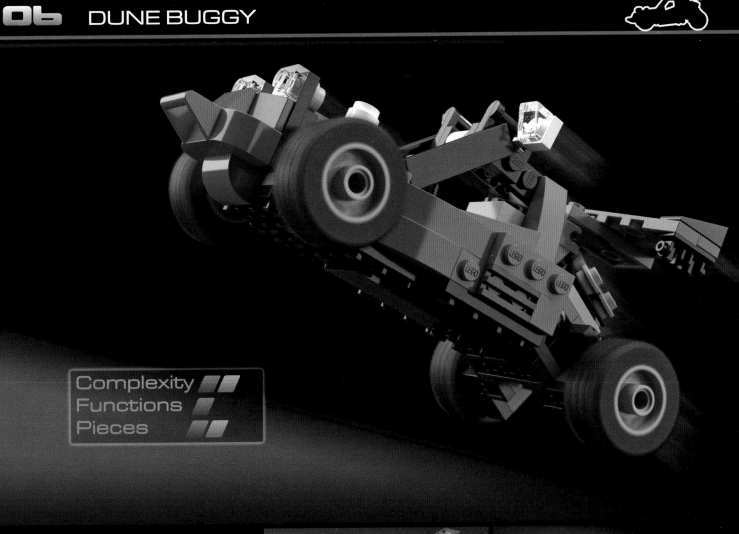

Complexity
Functions
Pieces

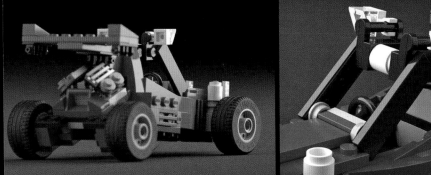

DUNE BUGGY

Design notes: roll cage, rear V4 engine, bull bar, exposed shocks, big rear wing, spotlights

Technical specifications:

Dimensions (l × w × h):	18 × 10 × 9 studs
Wheelbase:	12 studs
Axle width front/rear:	10/10 studs

Features: hinged rear axle

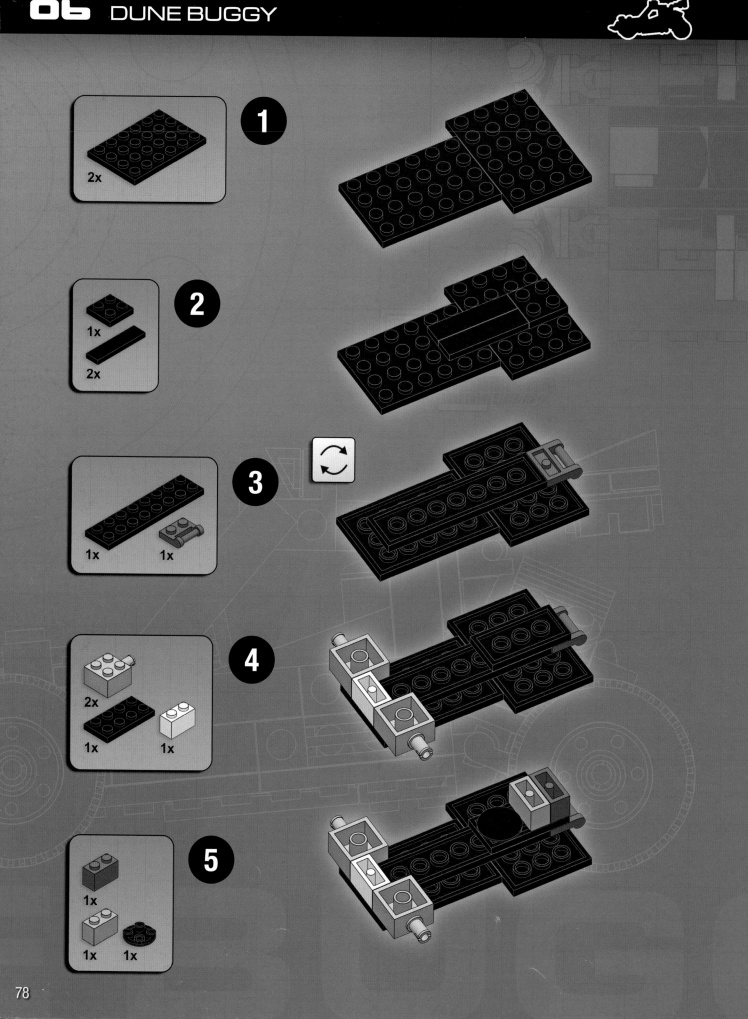

1
2x

2
1x
2x

3
1x 1x

4
2x
1x 1x

5
1x
1x 1x

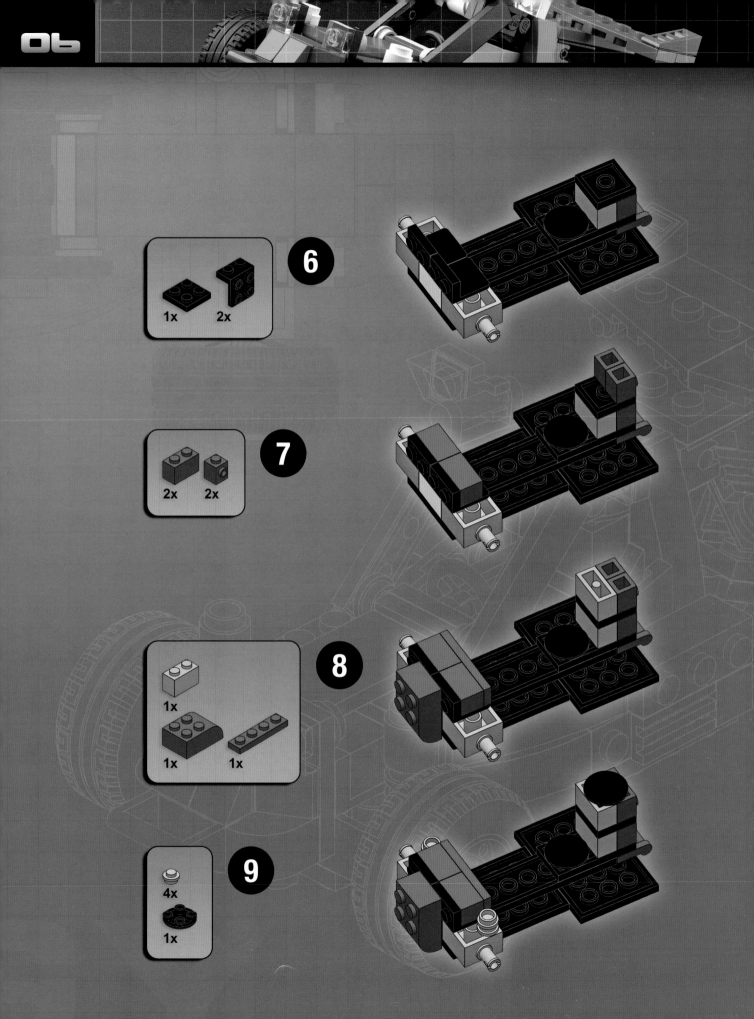

6

1x 2x

7

2x 2x

8

1x

1x 1x

9

4x

1x

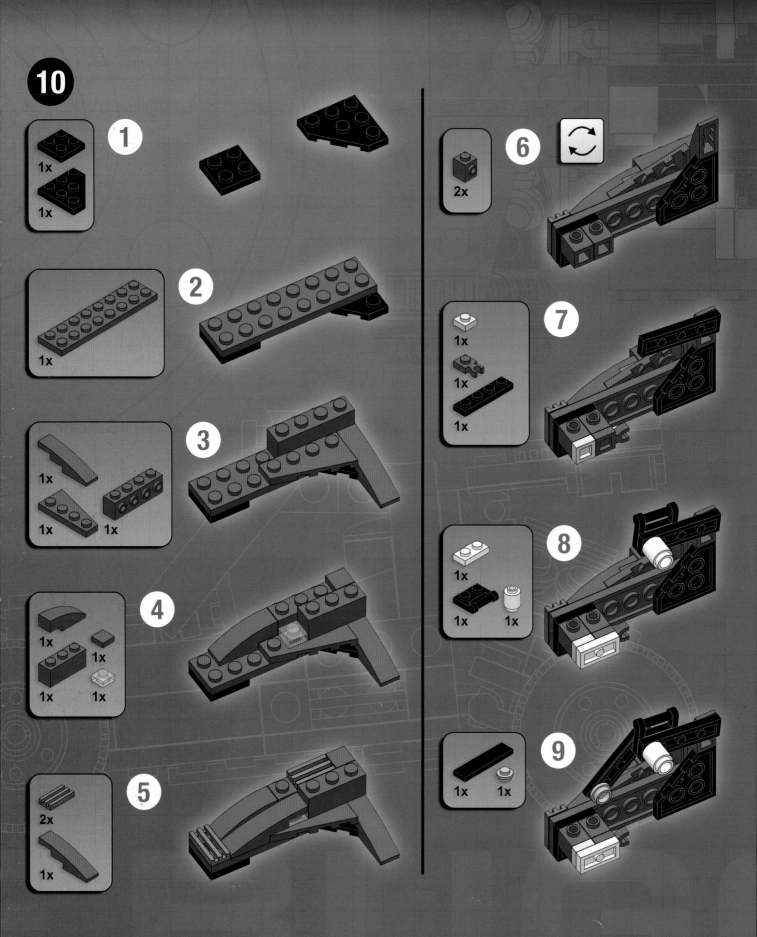

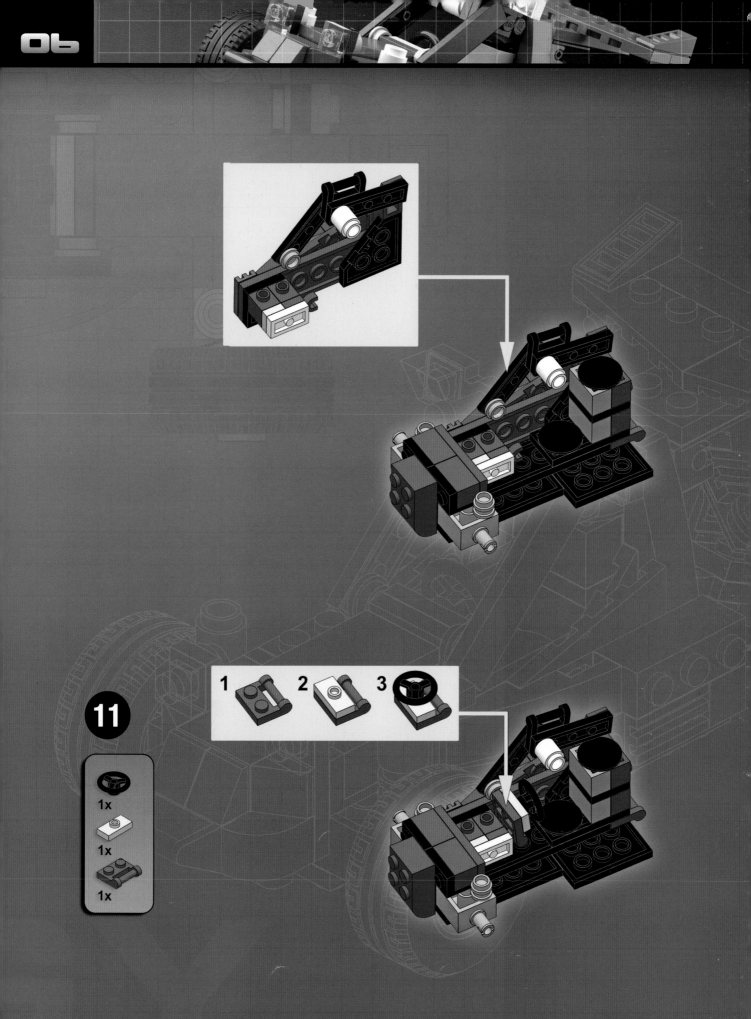

11

1 2 3

1x
1x
1x

12

1 1x 1x

2 1x

3 1x 1x

4 1x 1x

5 1x 1x 1x

6 2x 1x

7 1x

8 1x 1x

9 1x 1x

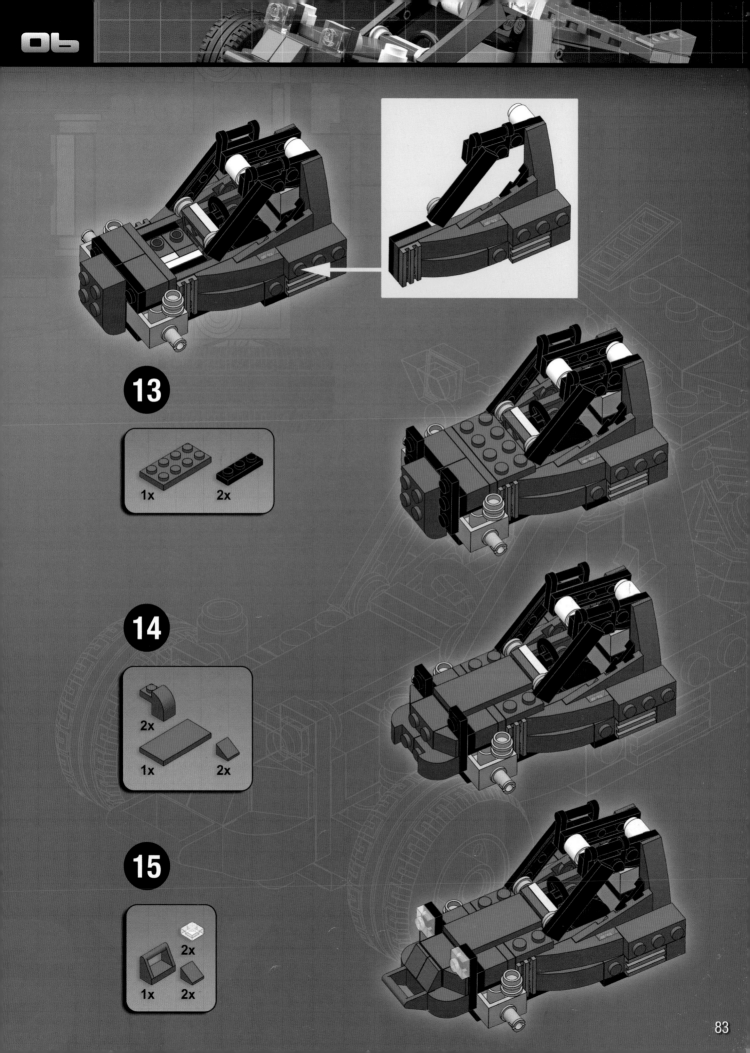

13

1x   2x

14

2x
1x   2x

15

2x
1x   2x

16

2x

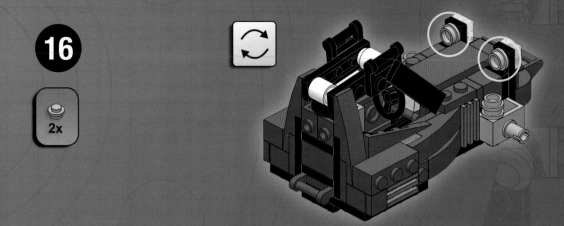

1

2

3

4

5

6

17

1x

1x

1x

1x

2x

2x

2x

1x

1x

1x

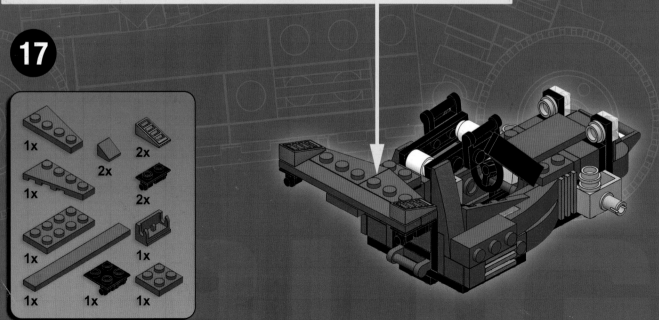

18

1
2x
1x

2
2x
2x

3
2x
1x   2x

4
1x
1x   2x

5
1x
2x   2x

6
2x
2x

7
2x
1x

8
2x
2x   1x

9
4x
2x

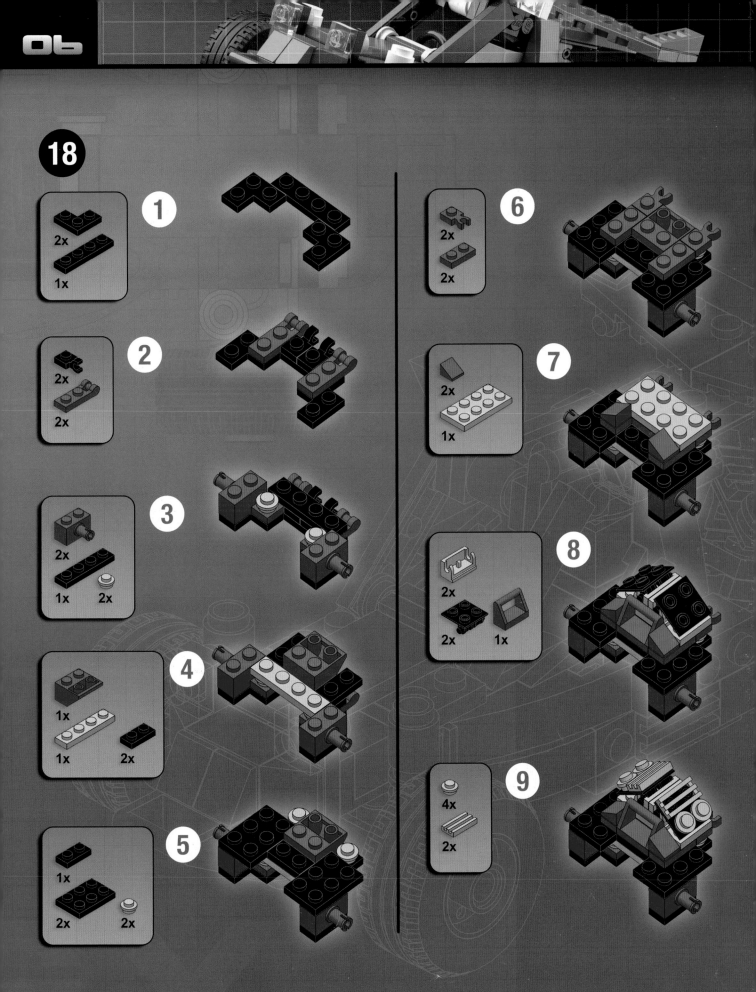

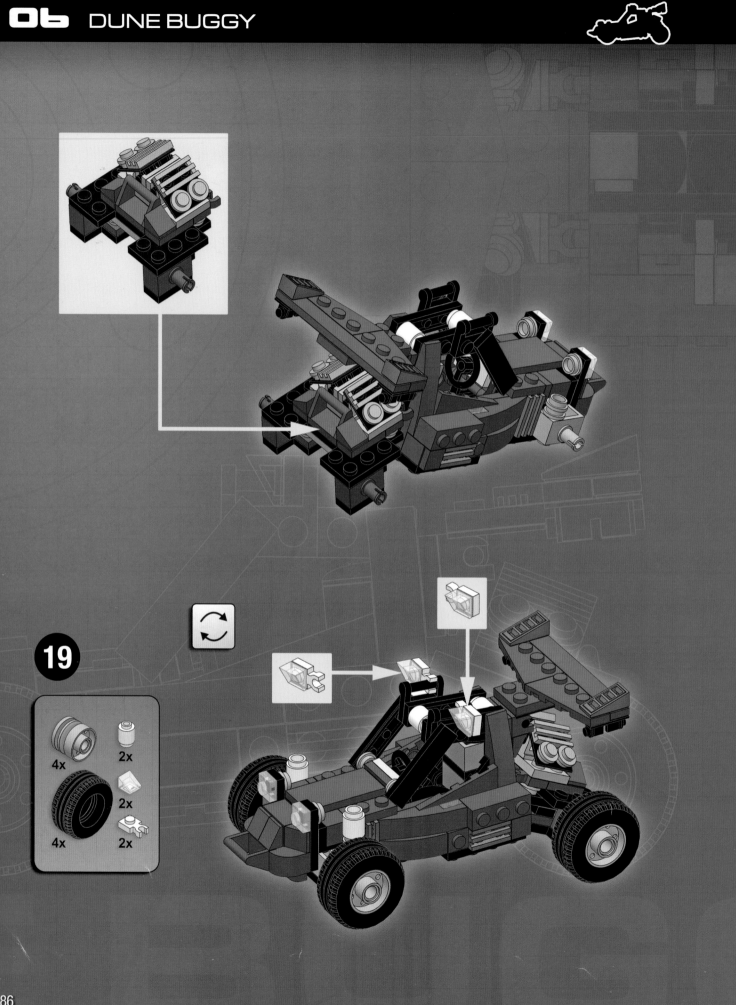

19

4x
2x
4x   2x
2x

Complexity

Functions

Pieces

FORKLIFT

Design notes: short wheelbase, open cabin, big mirrors, spotlights

Technical specifications:

Dimensions (l × w × h):	22 × 10 × 16 studs
Wheelbase:	9 studs
Axle width front/rear:	8/8 studs

Features: tilting mast, folding fork, pallet

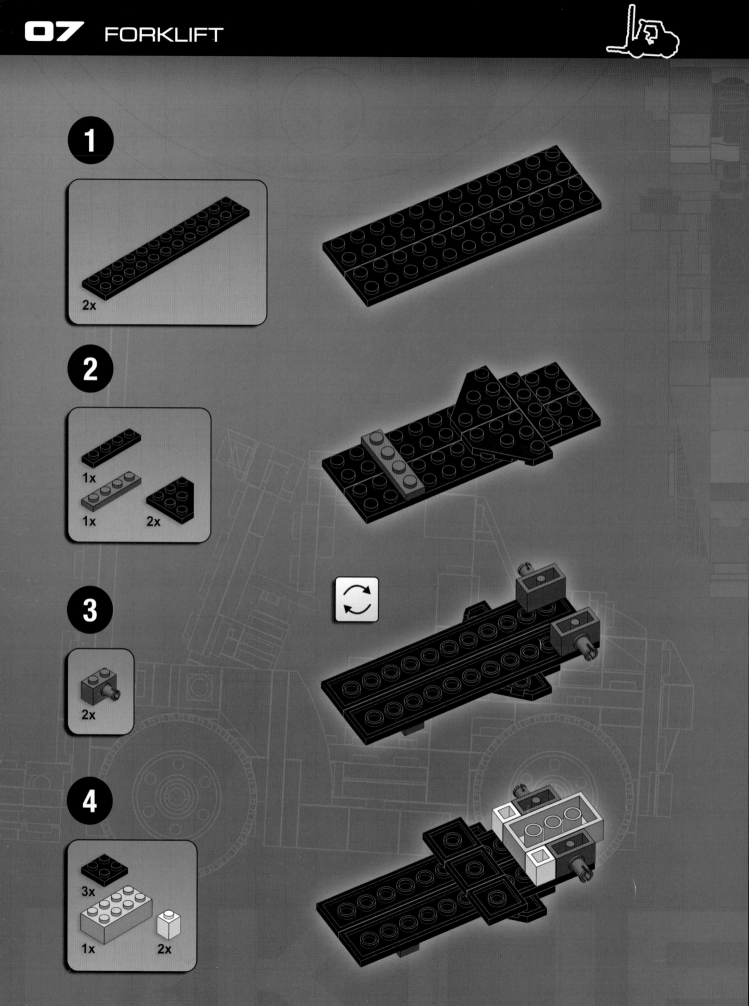

1

2x

2

1x
1x
2x

3

2x

4

3x
1x
2x

5

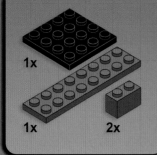

1x
1x
2x

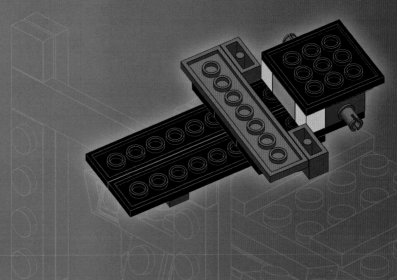

1
2
3

4
5

6

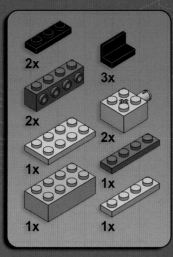

2x
3x
2x
2x
1x
1x
1x
1x

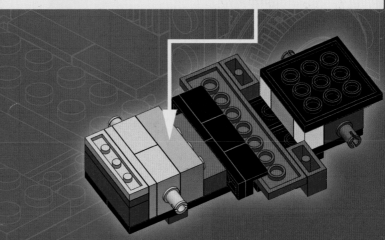

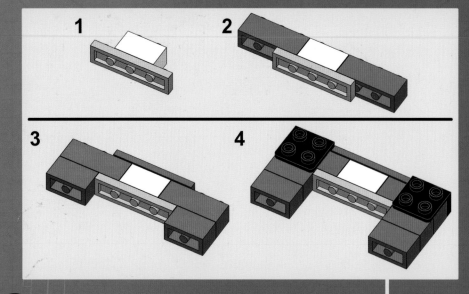

7

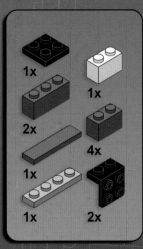

1x
1x
2x
4x
1x
1x
2x

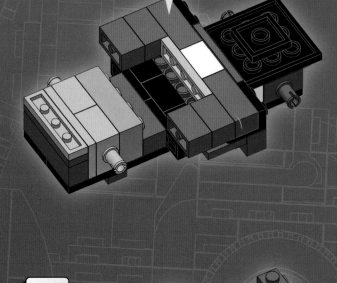

8

1x

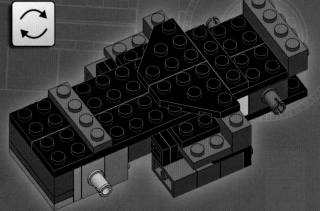

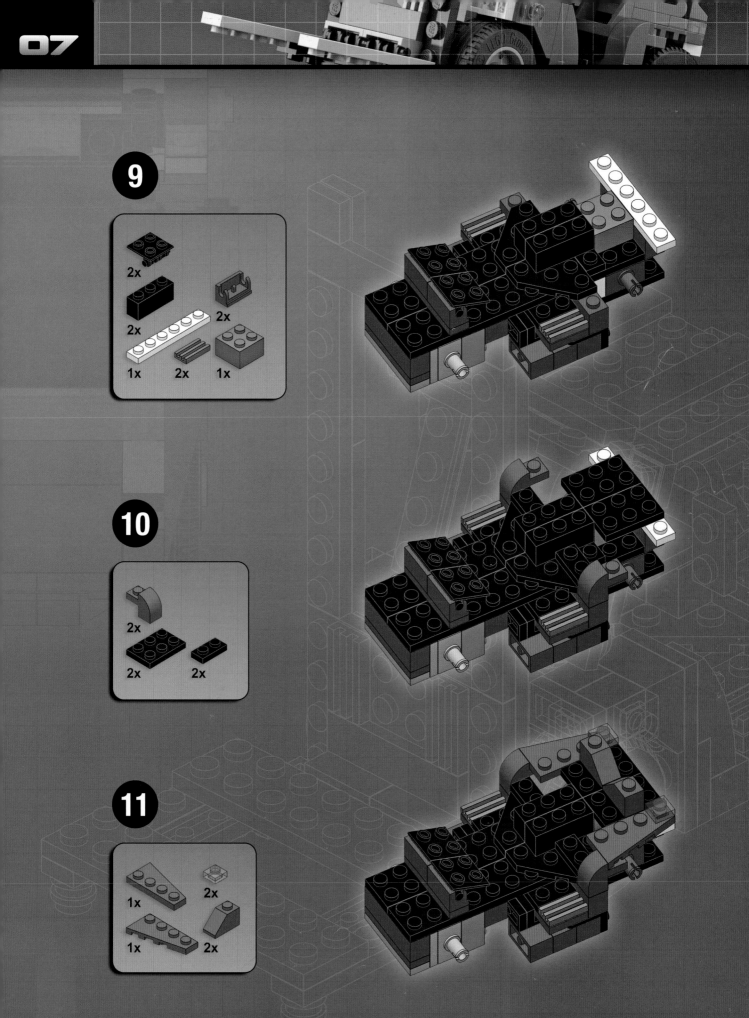

9

2x
2x
2x
1x
2x
1x

10

2x
2x
2x

11

1x
2x
1x
2x

12

2x
2x
2x
1x
2x

13

1x
2x
1x
2x

14

1x
2x
1x
1x
1x

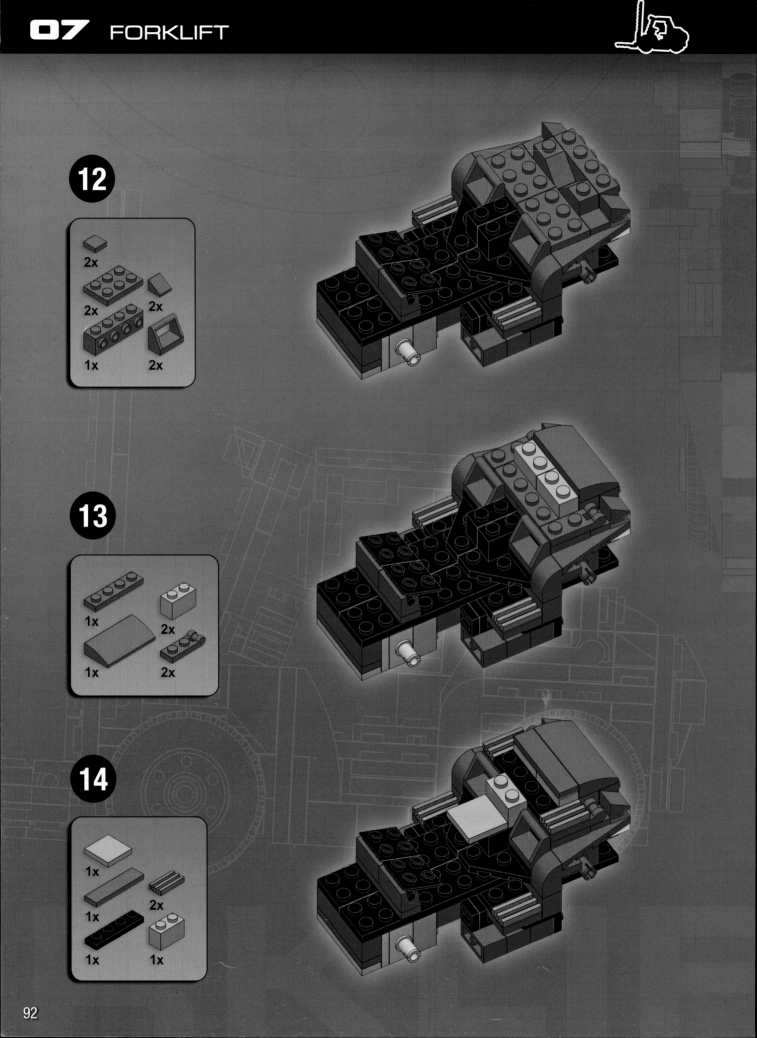

15

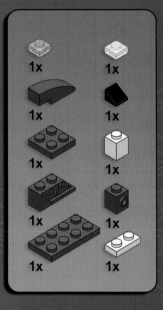

1x 1x
1x 1x
1x 1x
1x 1x
1x 1x

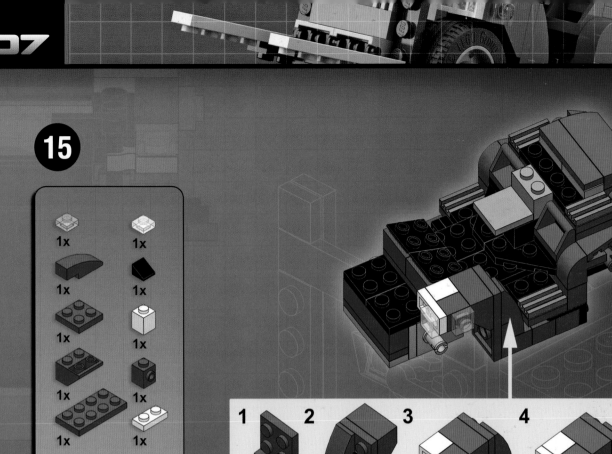

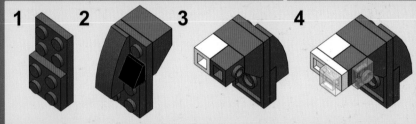

1   2   3   4

16

1x 1x
1x 1x
1x 1x
1x 1x
1x 1x

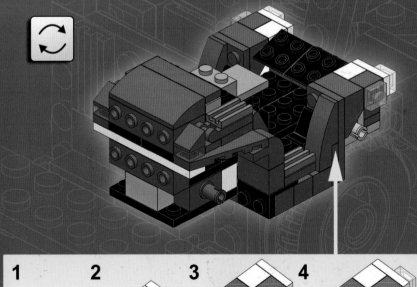

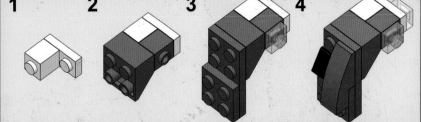

1   2   3   4

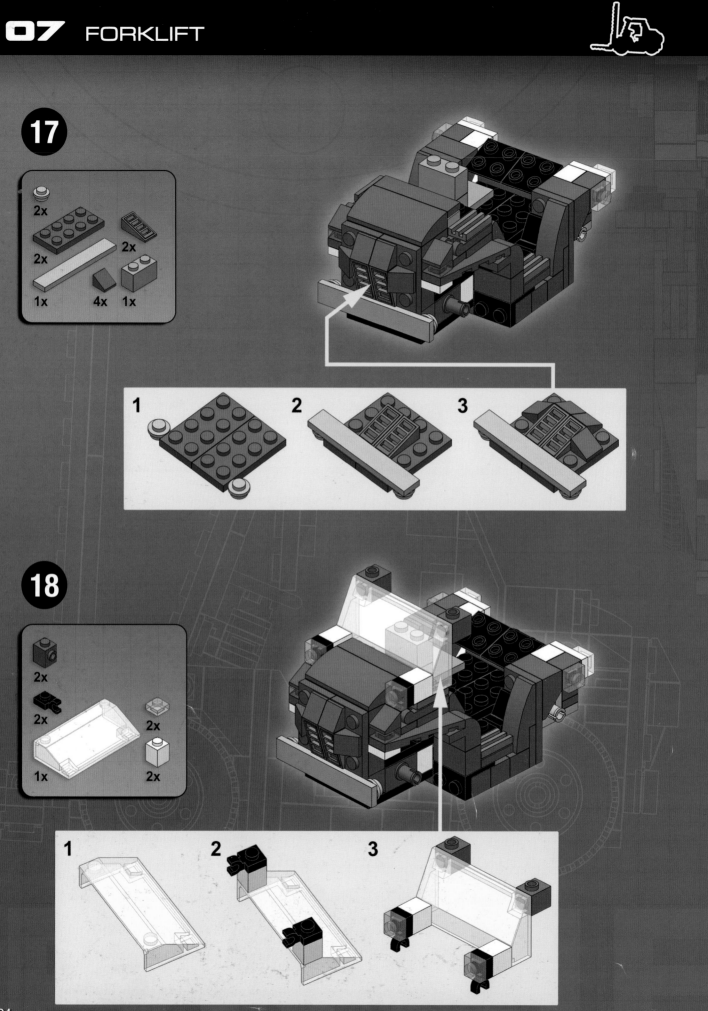

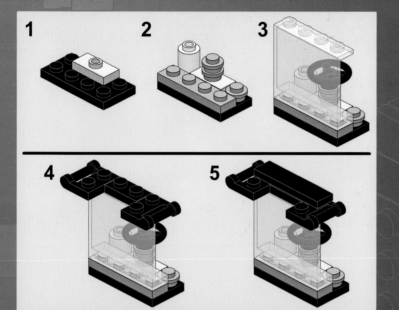

1
2
3

4
5

19

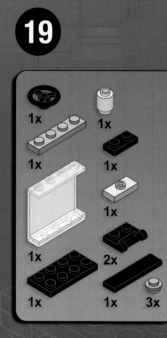

1x 1x
1x 1x
1x
1x 2x
1x 1x 3x

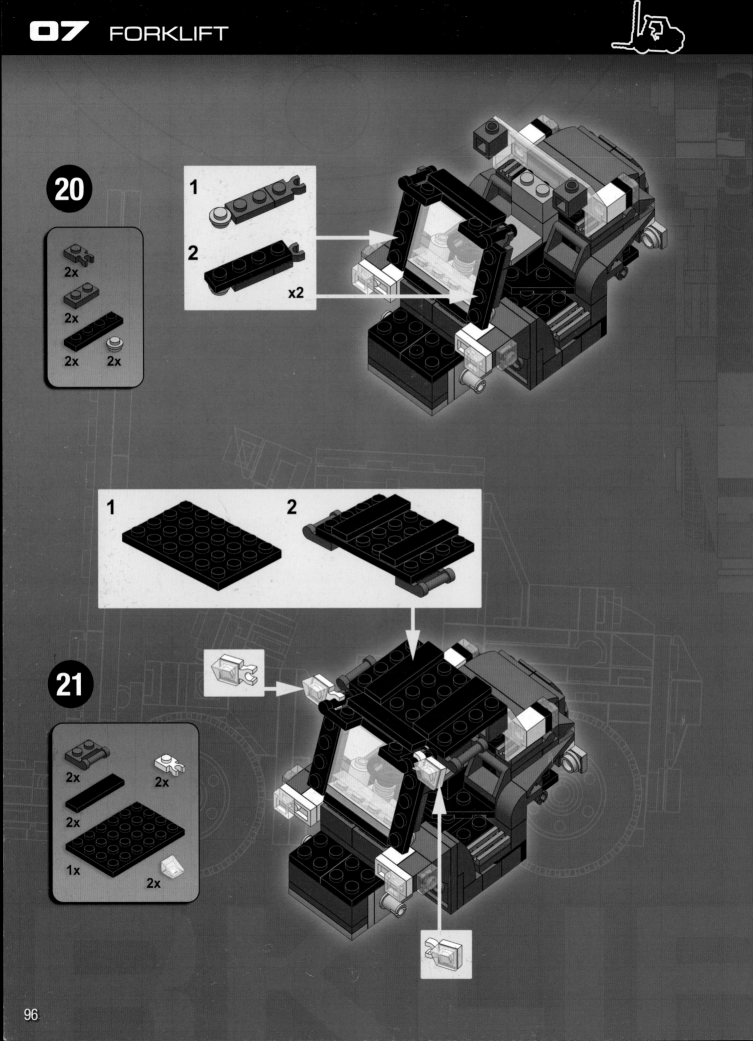

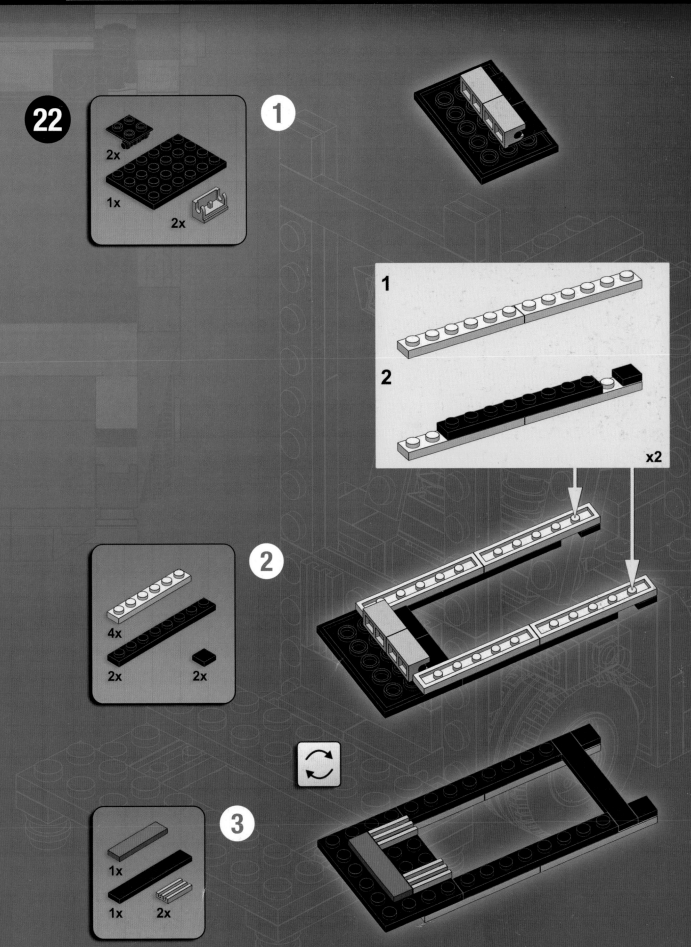

22

1
2x
1x
2x

1
2
x2

2
4x
2x
2x

3
1x
1x
2x

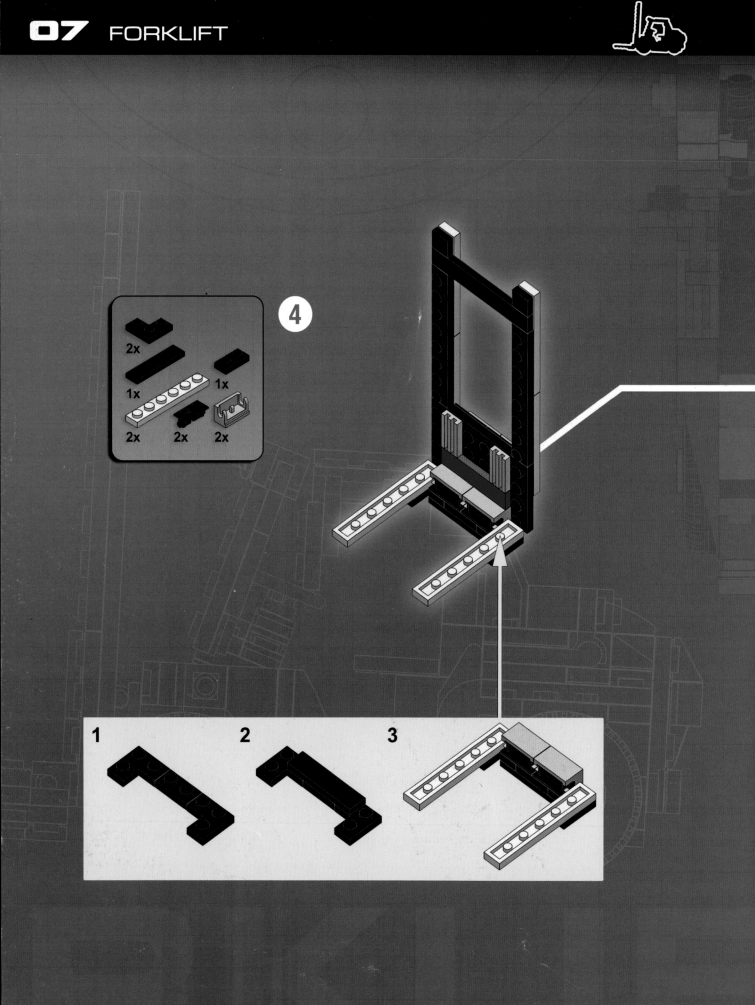

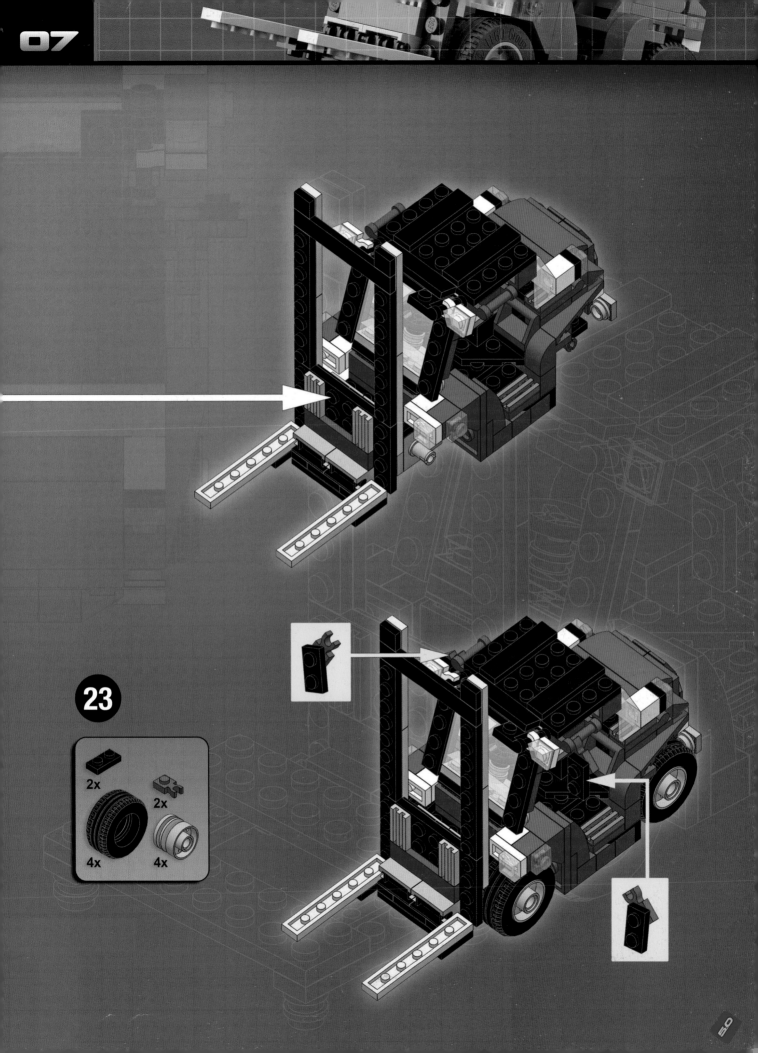

23

2x

2x

4x   4x

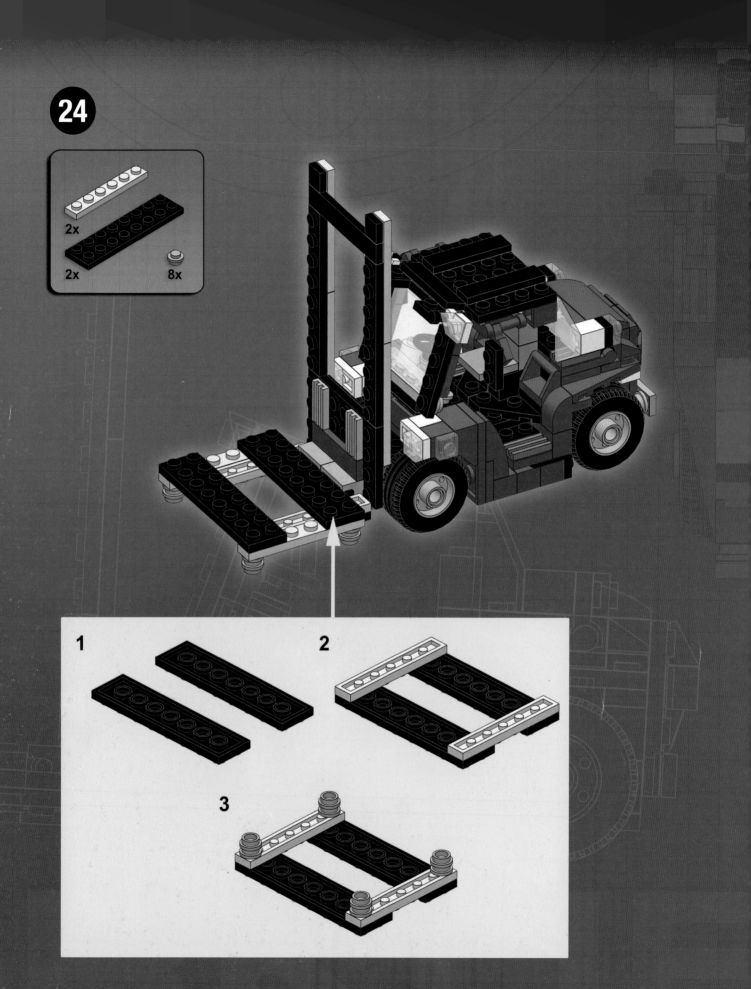

24

2x
2x
8x

1
2
3

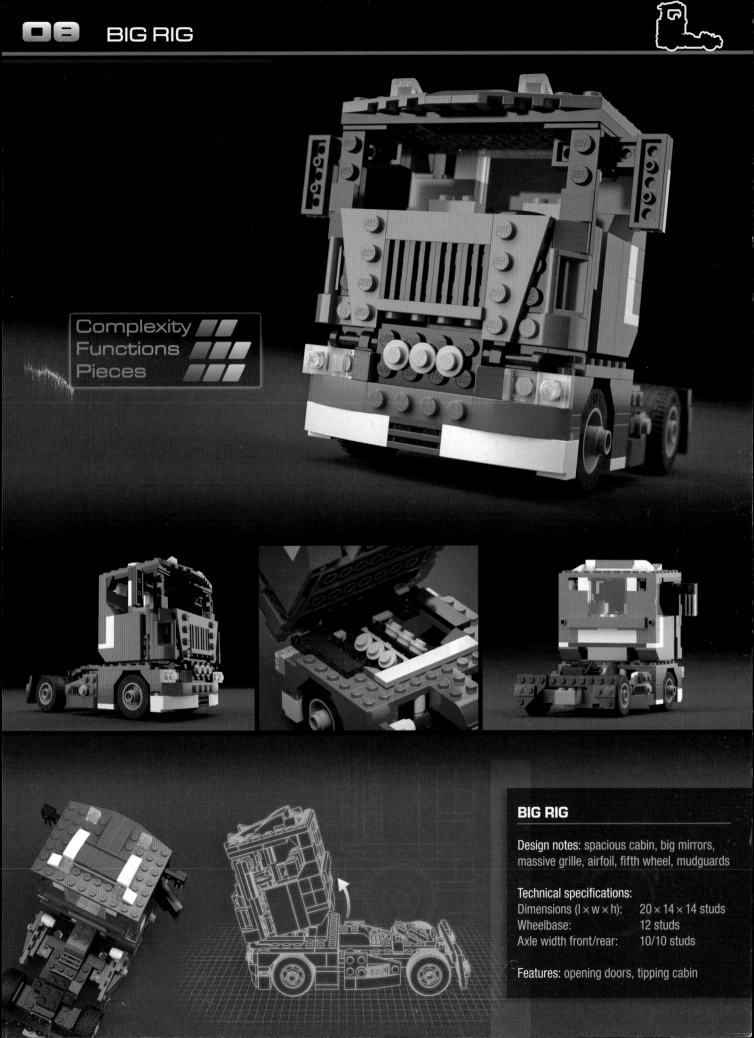

Complexity
Functions
Pieces

BIG RIG

Design notes: spacious cabin, big mirrors, massive grille, airfoil, fifth wheel, mudguards

Technical specifications:
Dimensions (l × w × h):   20 × 14 × 14 studs
Wheelbase: 12 studs
Axle width front/rear: 10/10 studs

Features: opening doors, tipping cabin

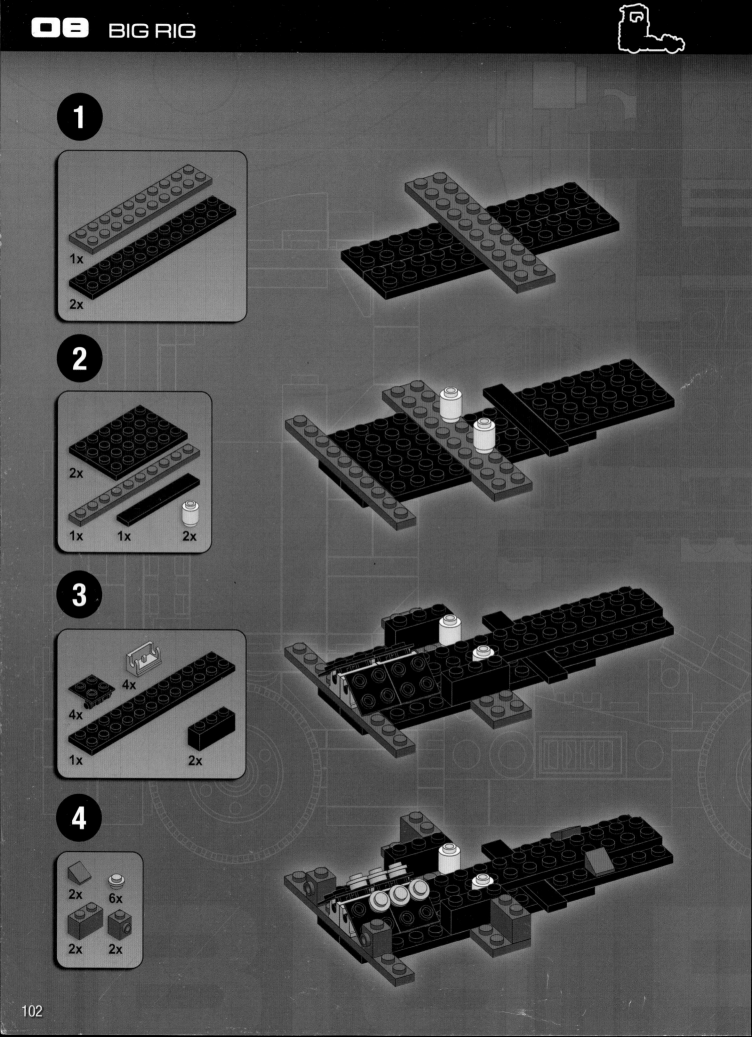

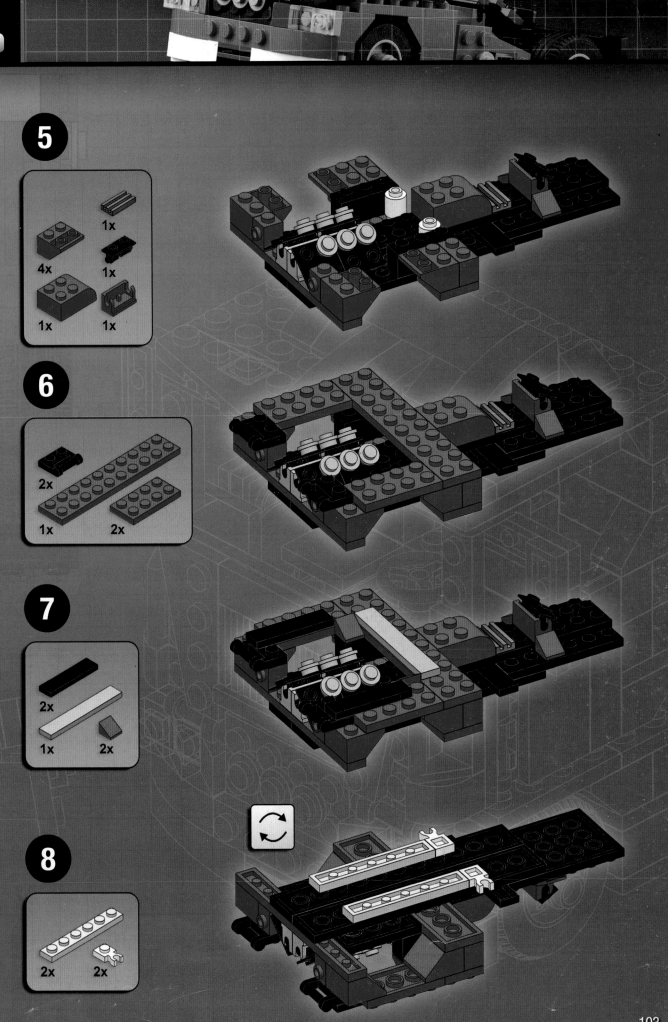

5

1x
4x
1x
1x
1x

6

2x
1x
2x

7

2x
1x
2x

8

2x
2x

9

1x
1x
2x   2x

10

4x
2x
1x

11

2x
1x
1x   2x

12

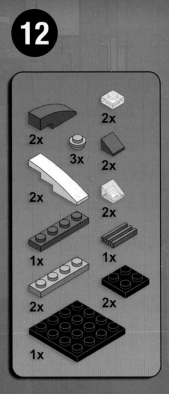

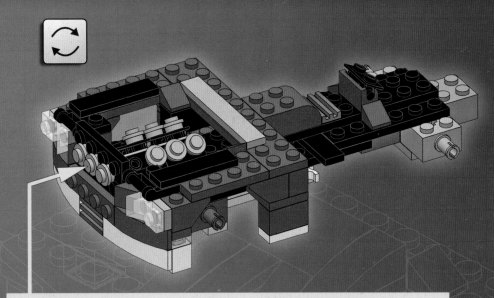

1

2

3

4

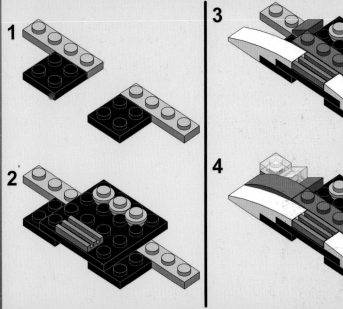

13

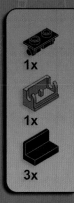

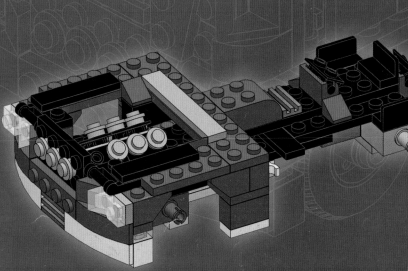

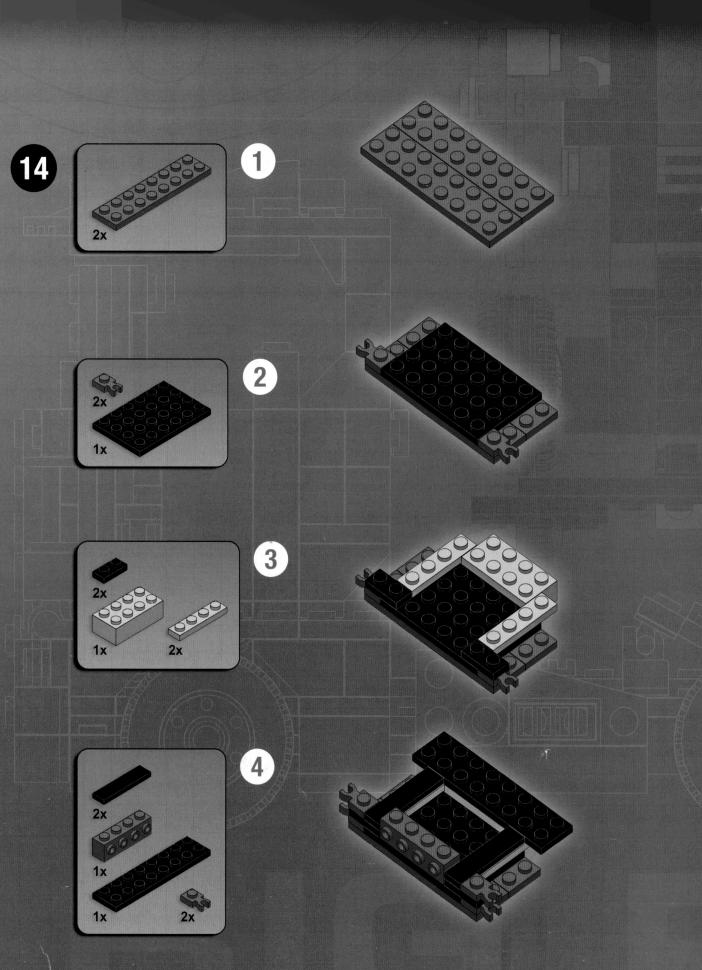

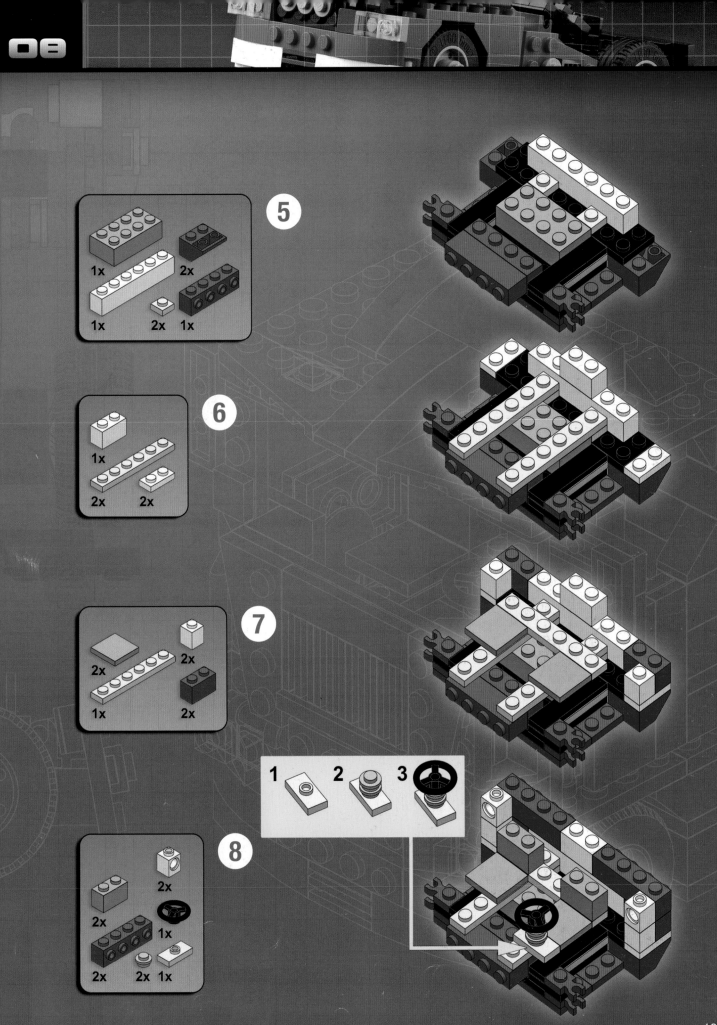

5

1x
2x
1x
2x
1x

6

1x
2x
2x

7

2x
2x
1x
2x

1
2
3

8

2x
2x
2x
1x
2x
2x
1x

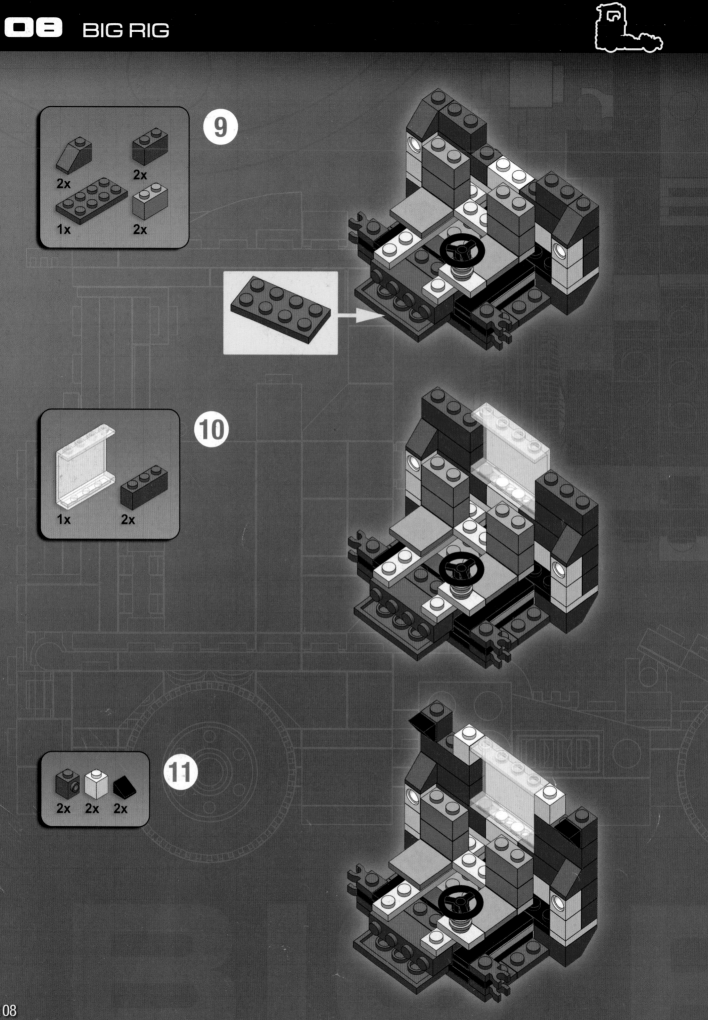

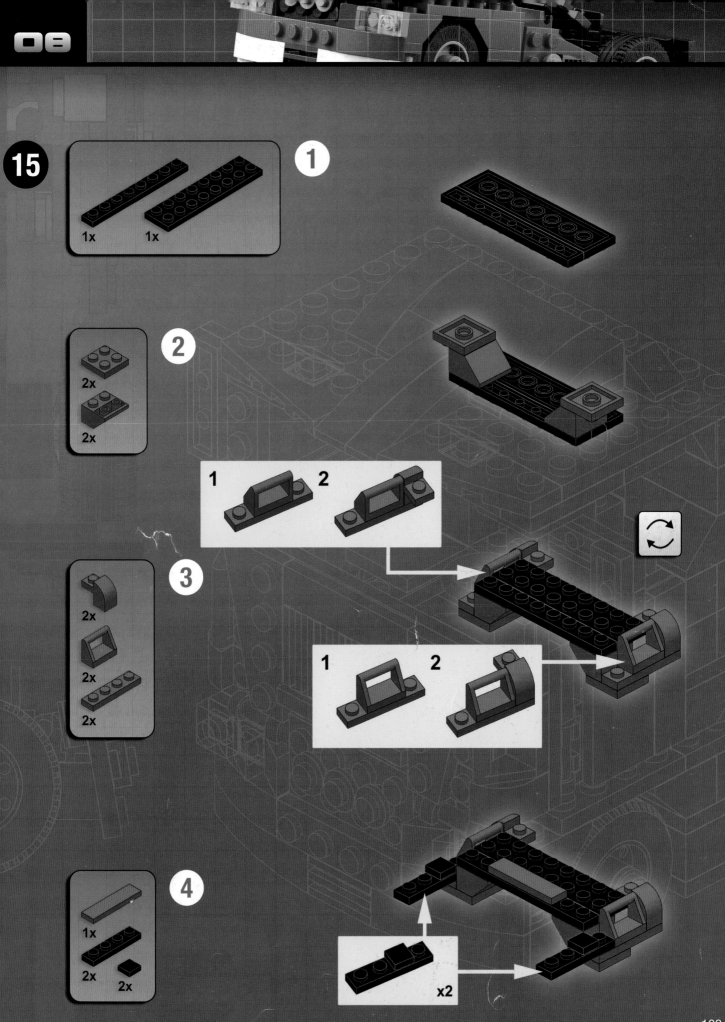

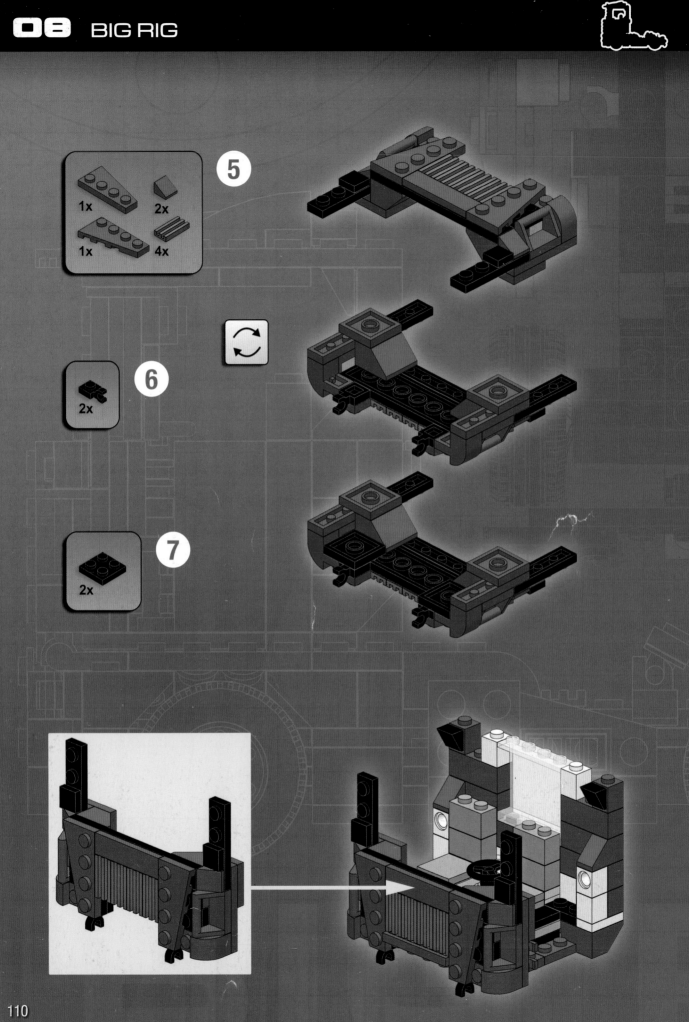

16

1
1x
1x   1x

2
4x
2x
1x

3
2x
1x   4x

4
2x   2x
1x   2x

5
2x
2x

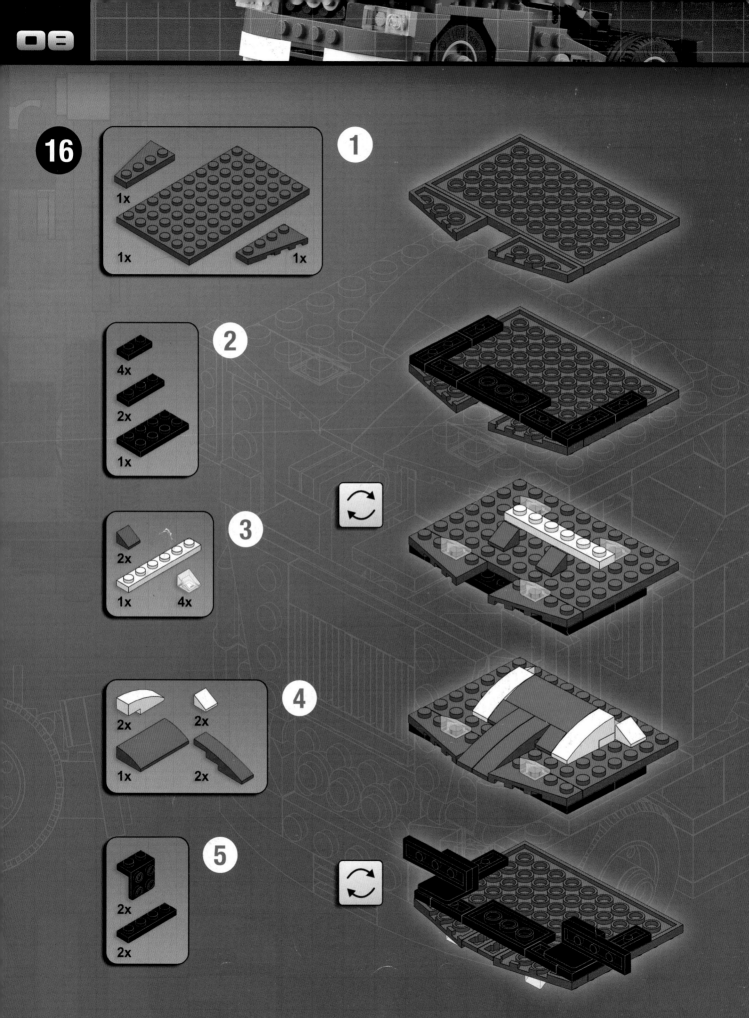

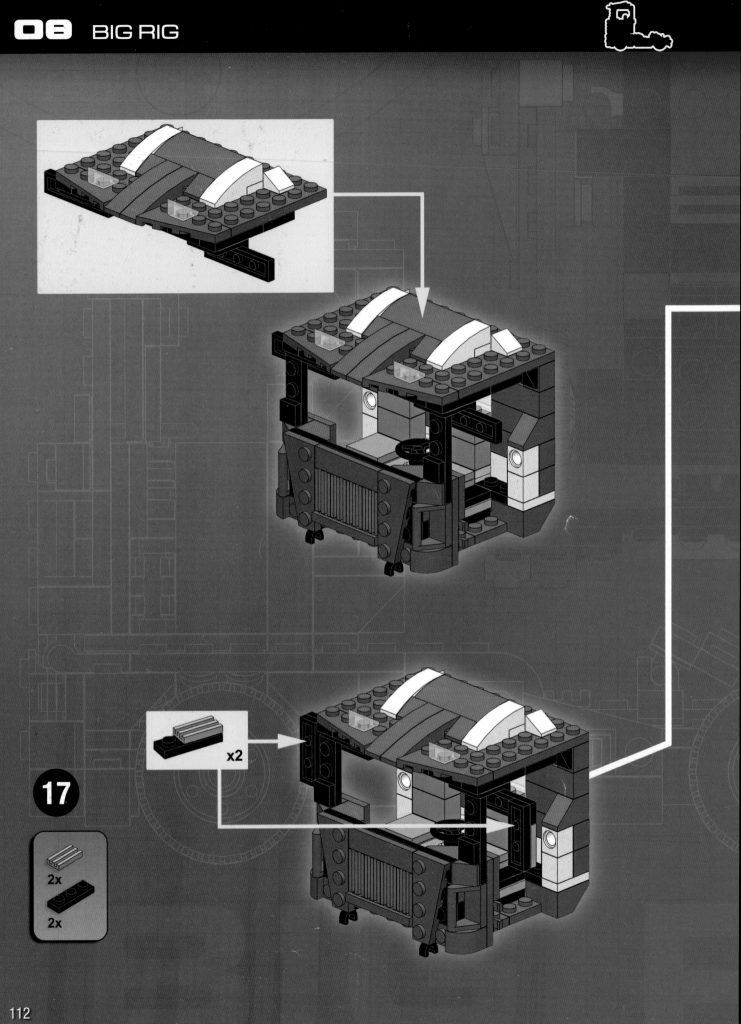

17

2x
2x

x2

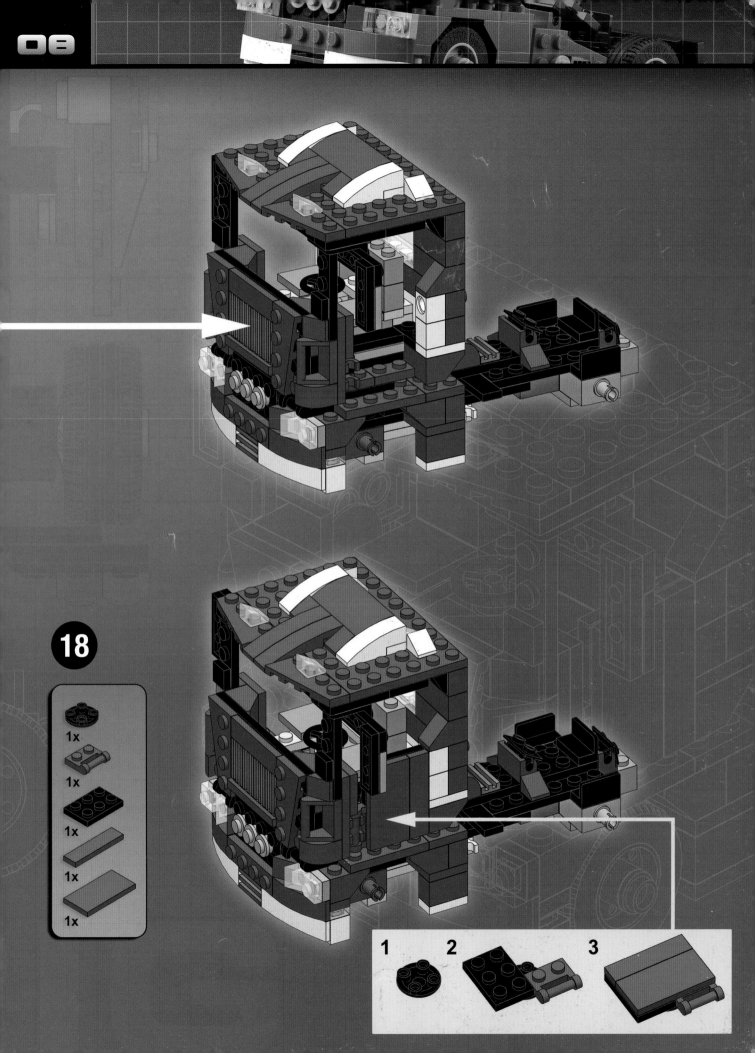

18

1x
1x
1x
1x
1x

1   2   3

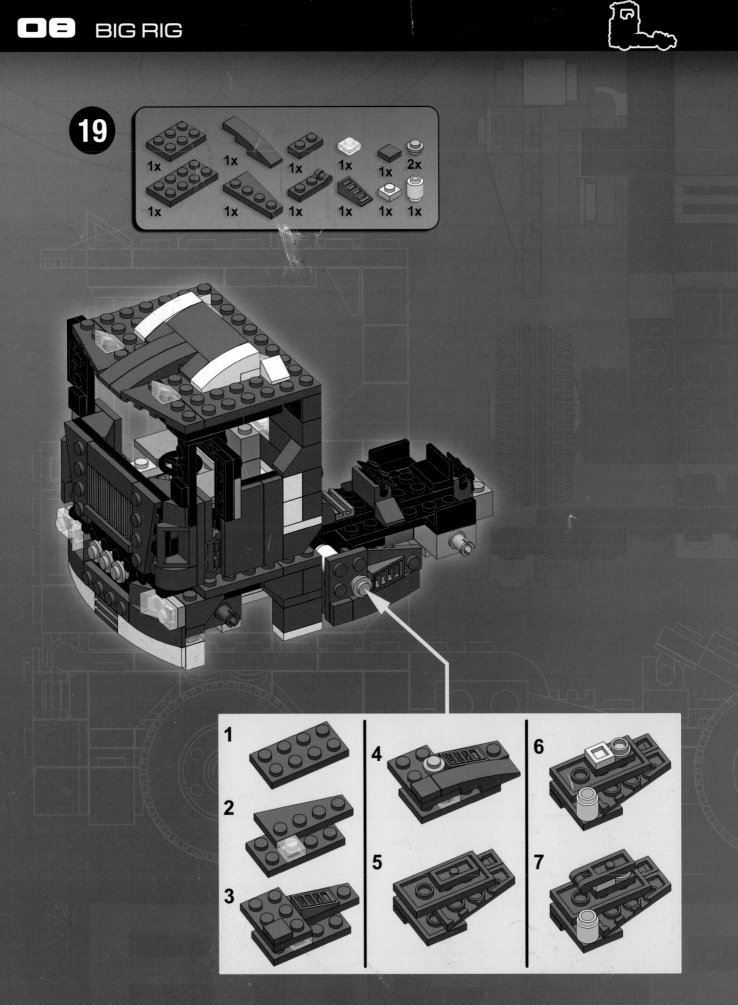

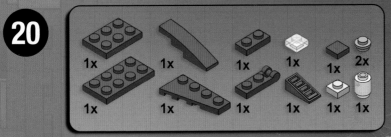

20

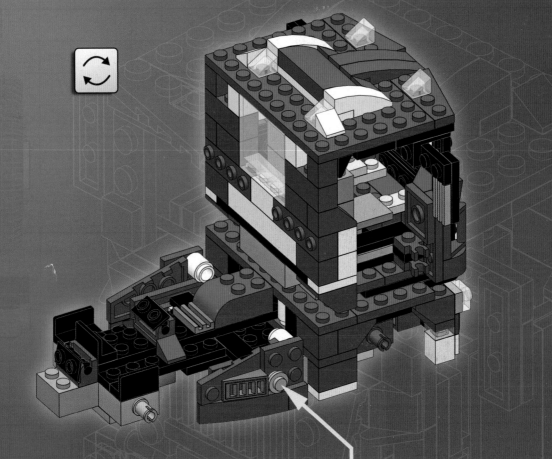

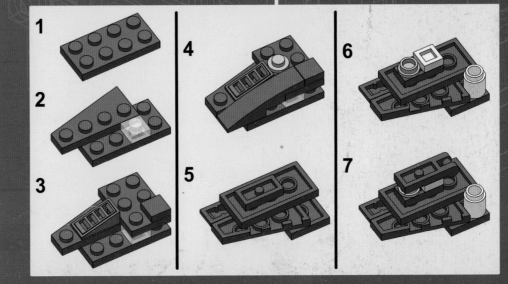

1

2

3

4

5

6

7

21

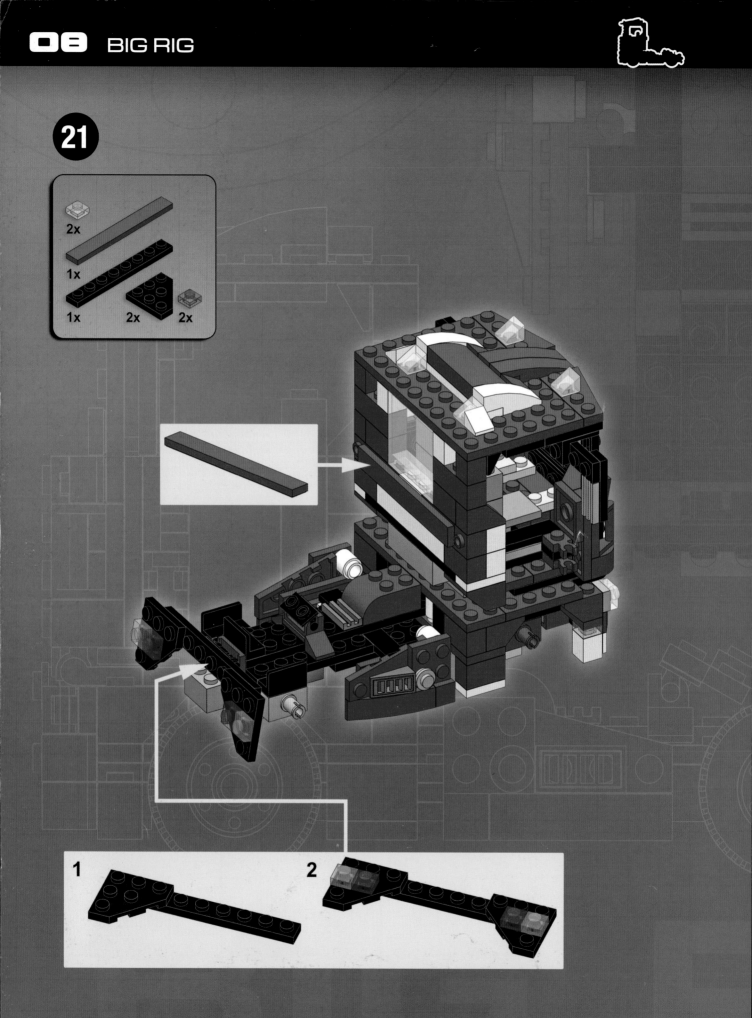

1

2

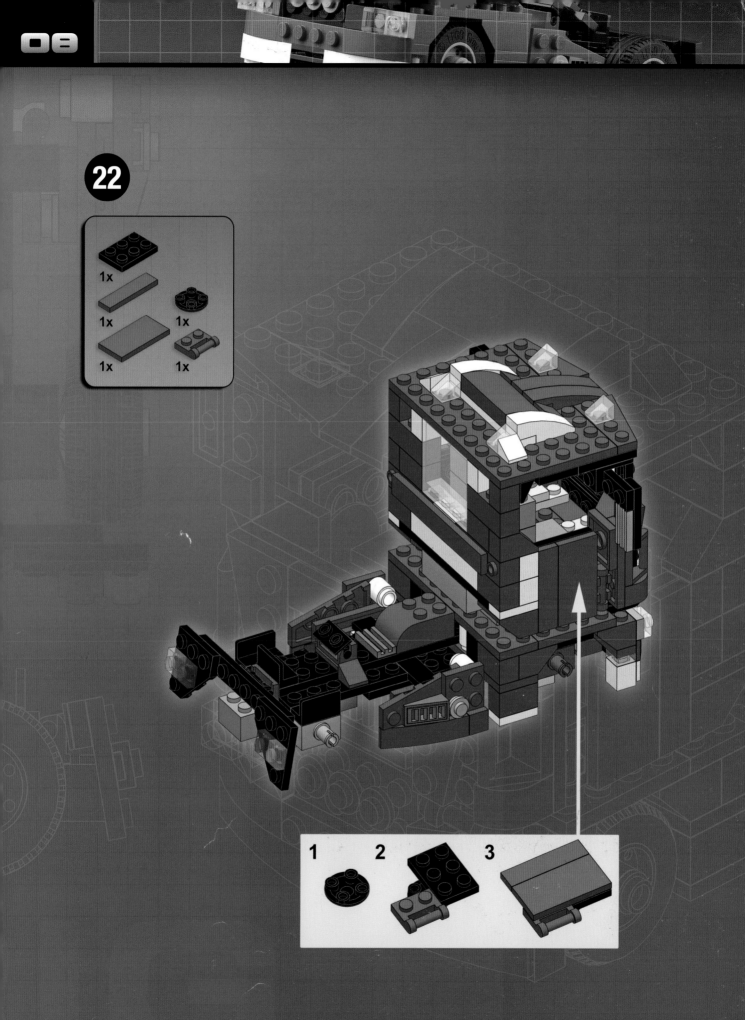

23

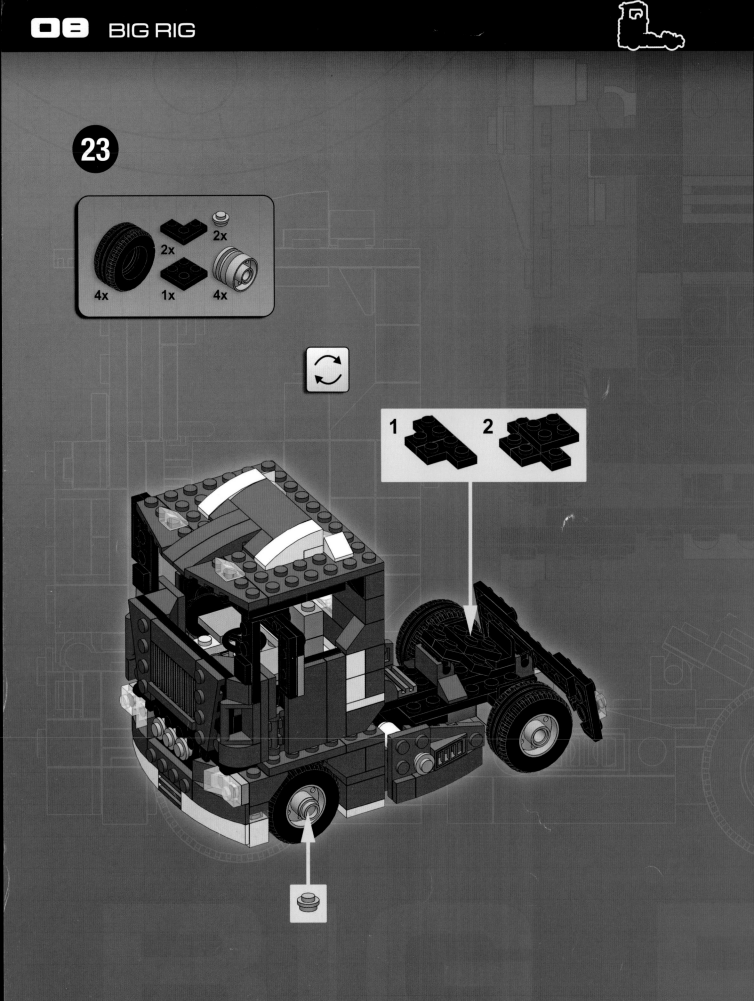

Complexity
Functions
Pieces

F1 RACER

Design notes: low chassis, aerodynamic shape, open-wheeled design, air intakes, front and rear wings

Technical specifications:
Dimensions (l × w × h):	27 × 10 × 8 studs
Wheelbase:	17 studs
Axle width front/rear:	10/10 studs

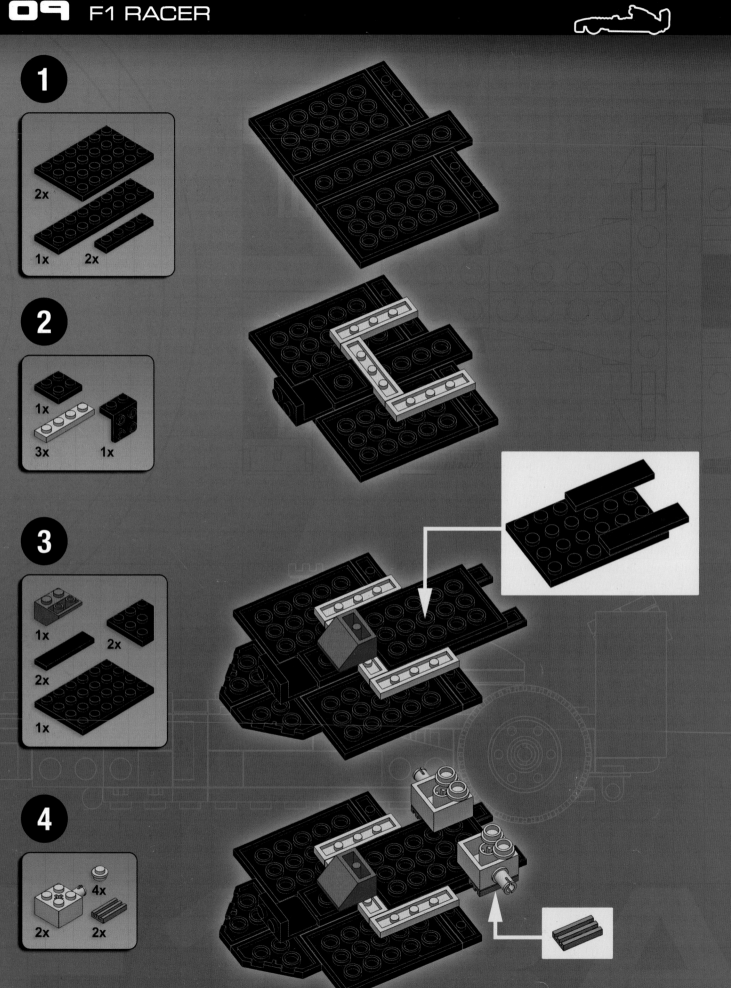

1

2x
1x 2x

2

1x
3x 1x

3

1x
2x
2x
1x

4

4x
2x 2x

5

1 1x

2 1x 1x 1x

3 2x 1x

4 1x 2x 2x

5 1x 1x 1x

6 1x 1x 1x

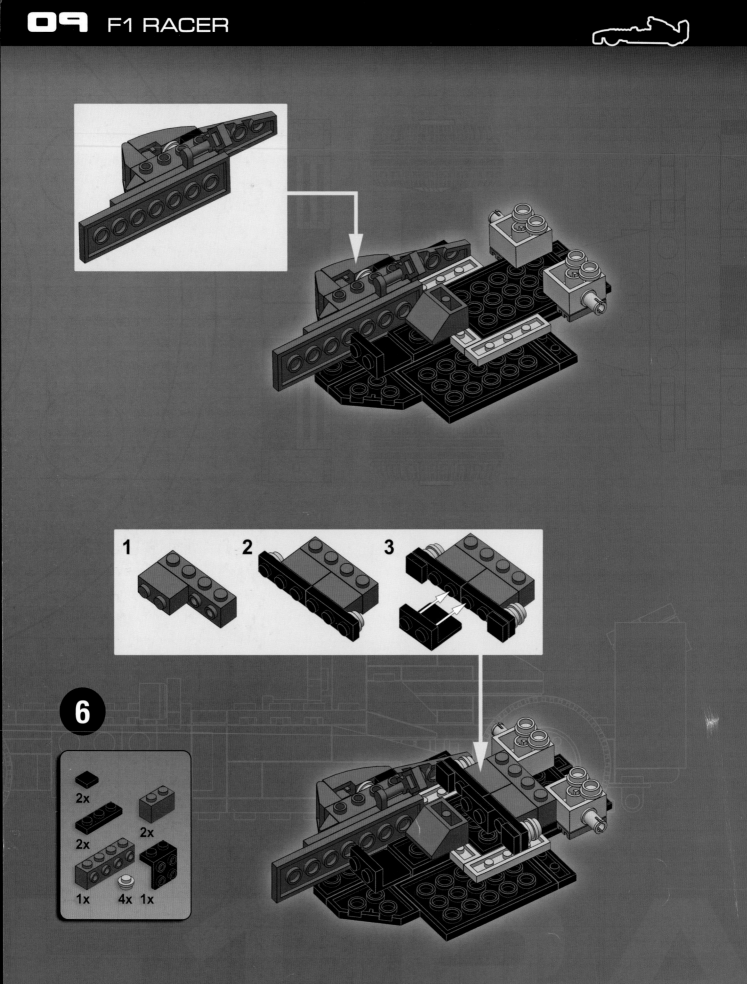

1

2

3

6

2x

2x

2x

1x 4x 1x

7

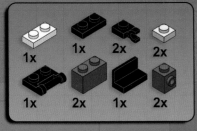

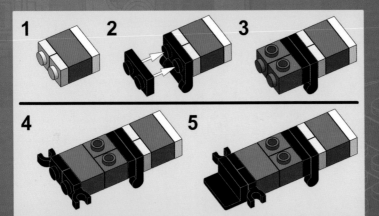

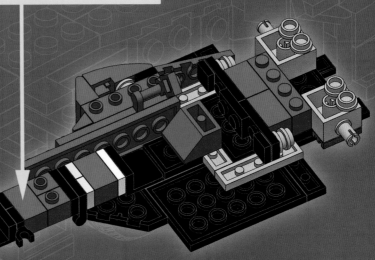

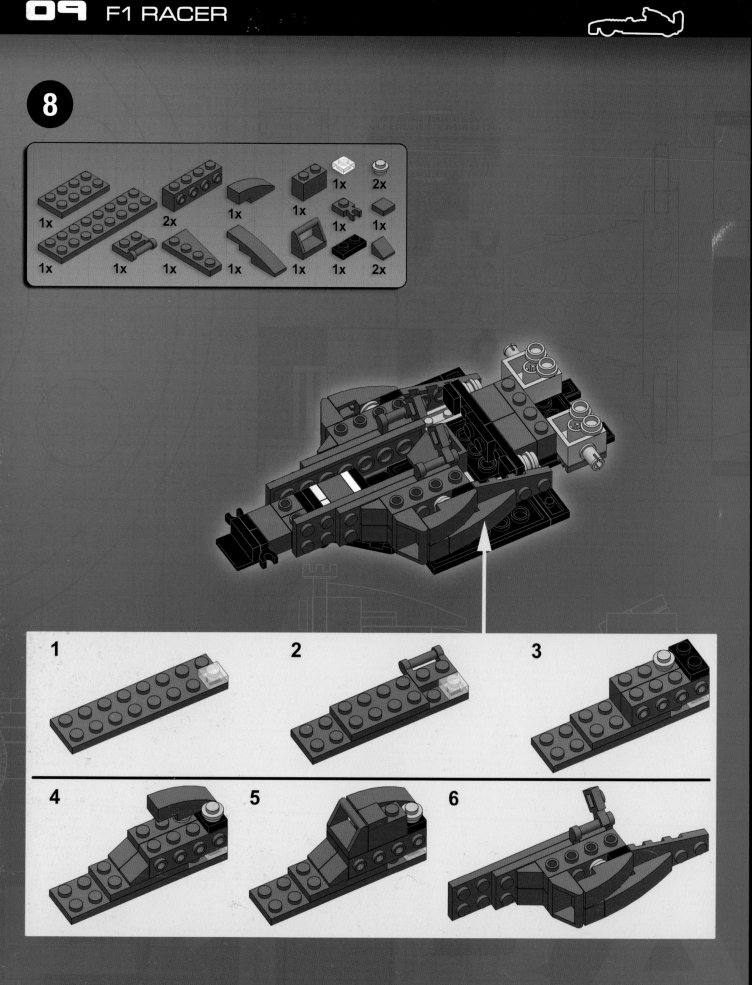

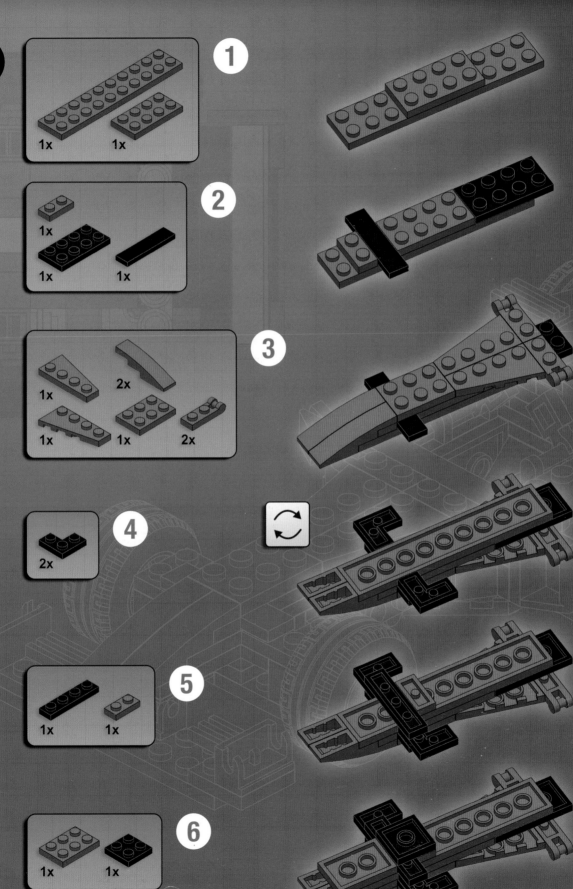

7

2x 1x

8

2x 2x

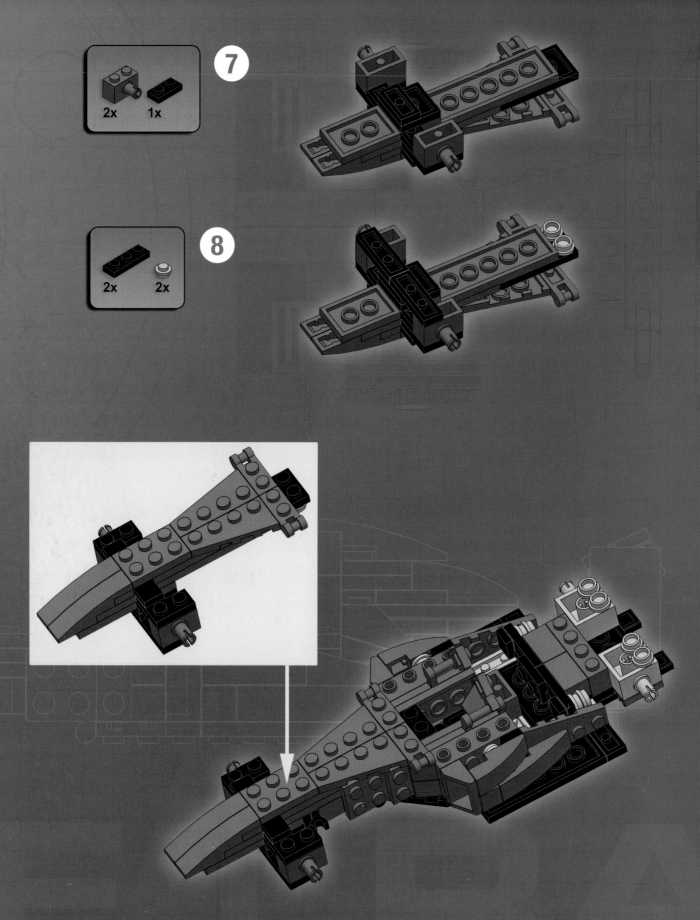

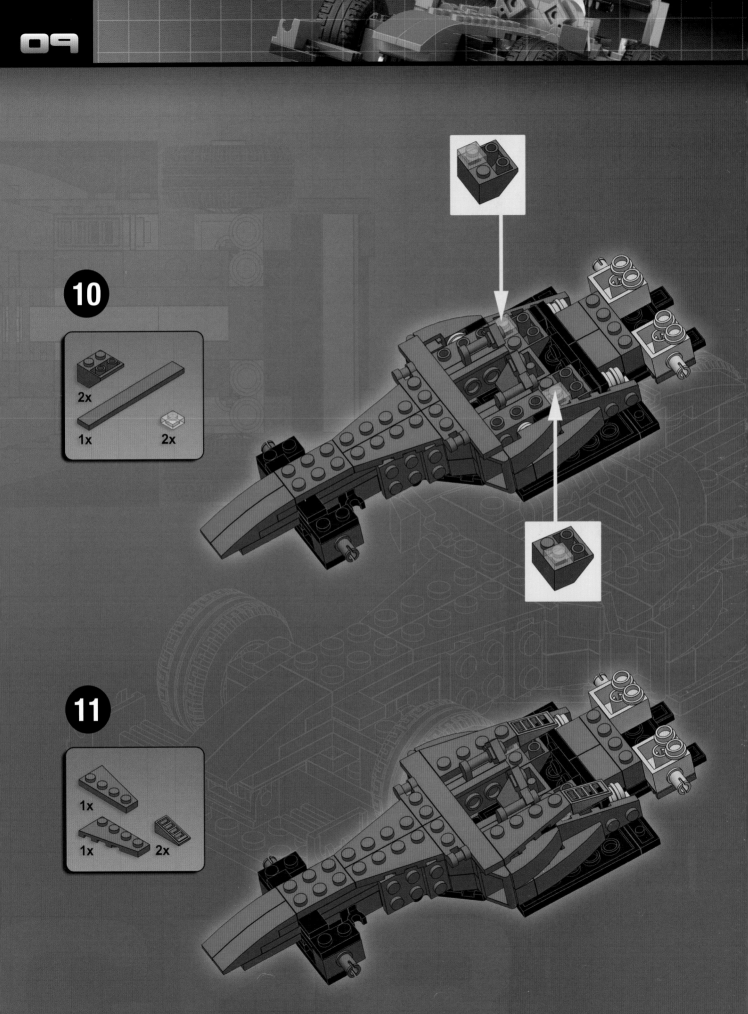

12

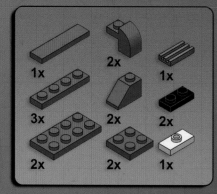

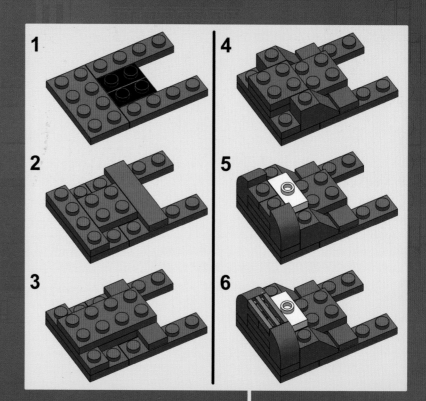

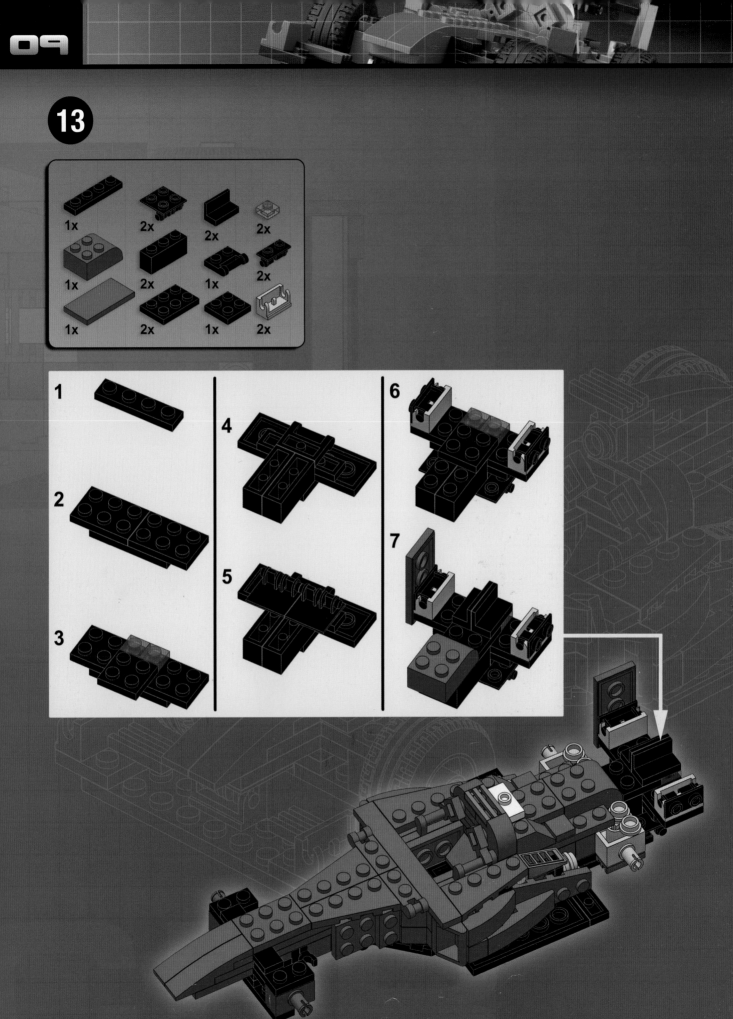

14

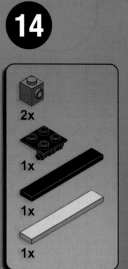

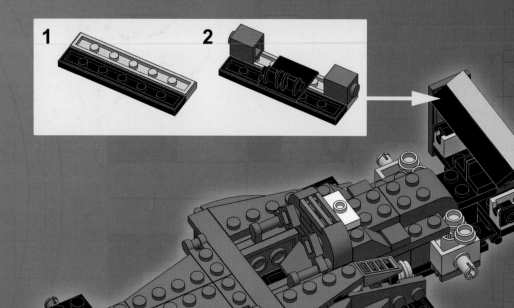

15

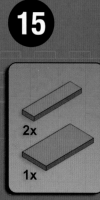

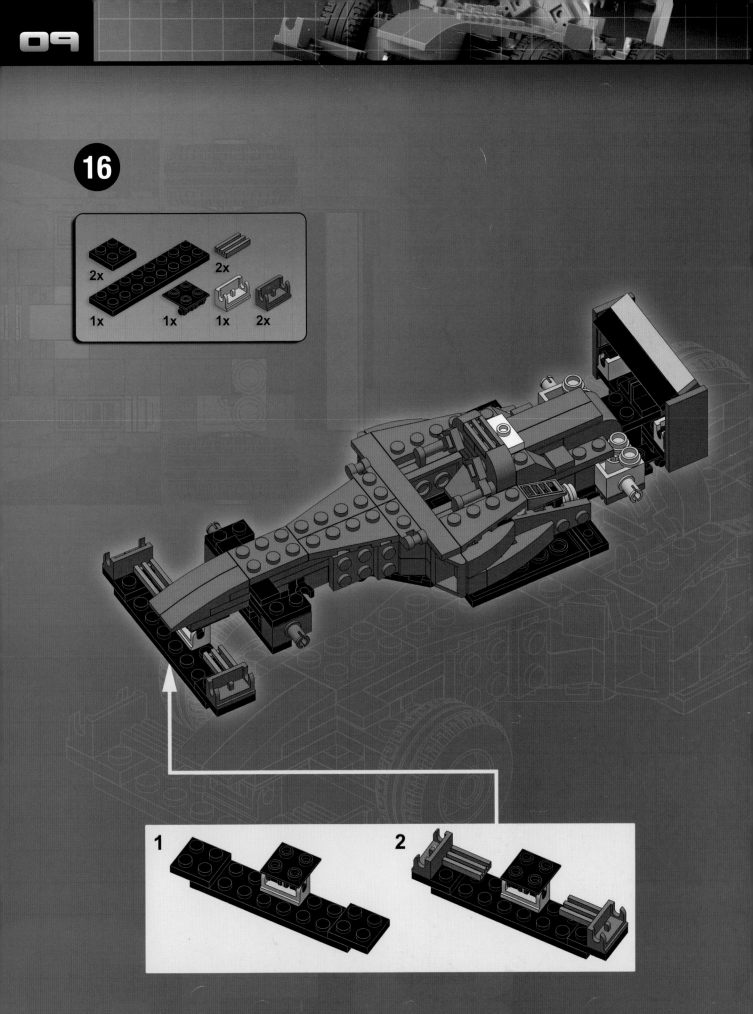

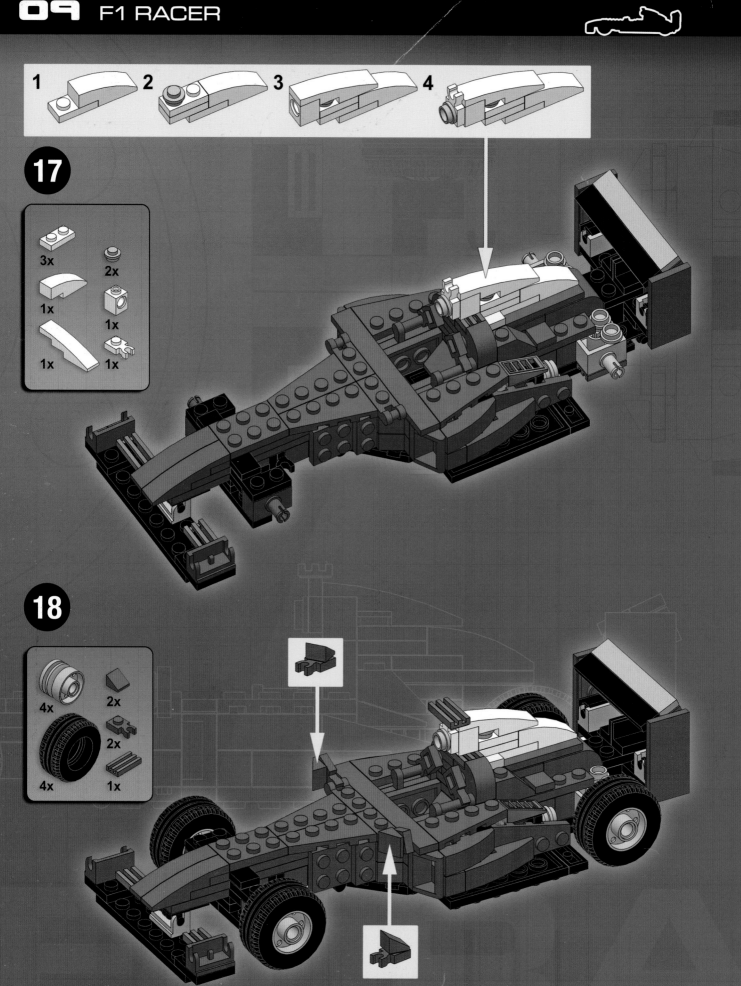

Complexity
Functions
Pieces

EXCAVATOR

Design notes: short wheelbase, high clearance, offset cabin, vertical exhaust, hazard light

Technical specifications:
Dimensions (l × w × h): 17 × 9 × 16 studs
Wheelbase: 9 studs
Axle width front/rear: 8/8 studs

Features: rotating turret; front blade; articulated arm, dipper, and bucket

1

2x
2x

2

2x
1x
1x
2x

3

2x
2x
1x
1x

4

1x
1x
1x
1x
1x

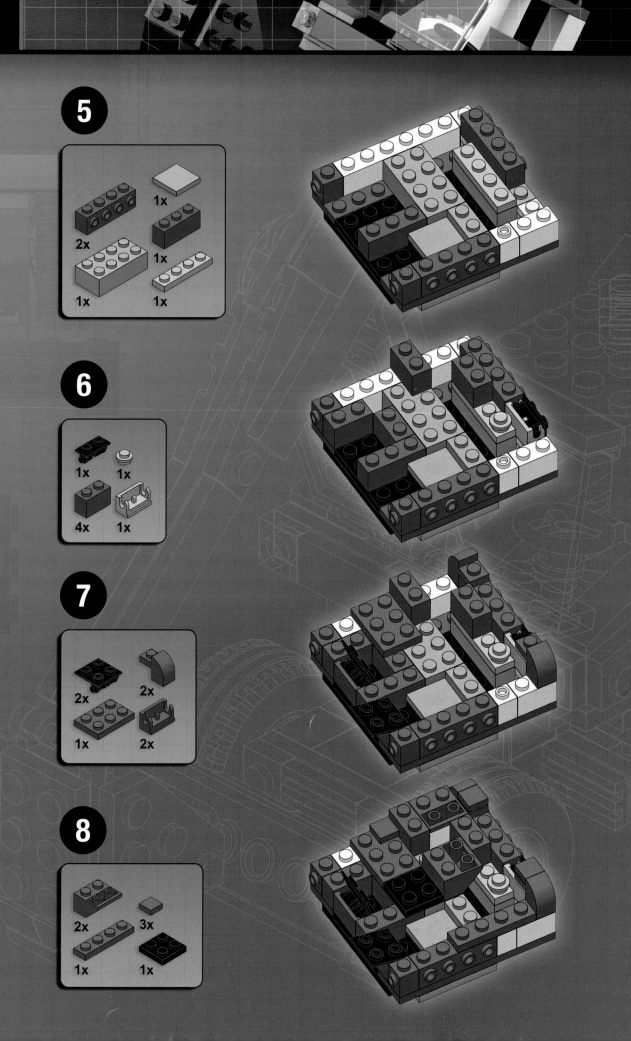

5

1x
2x
1x
1x

6

1x
1x
4x
1x

7

2x
2x
1x
2x

8

2x
3x
1x
1x

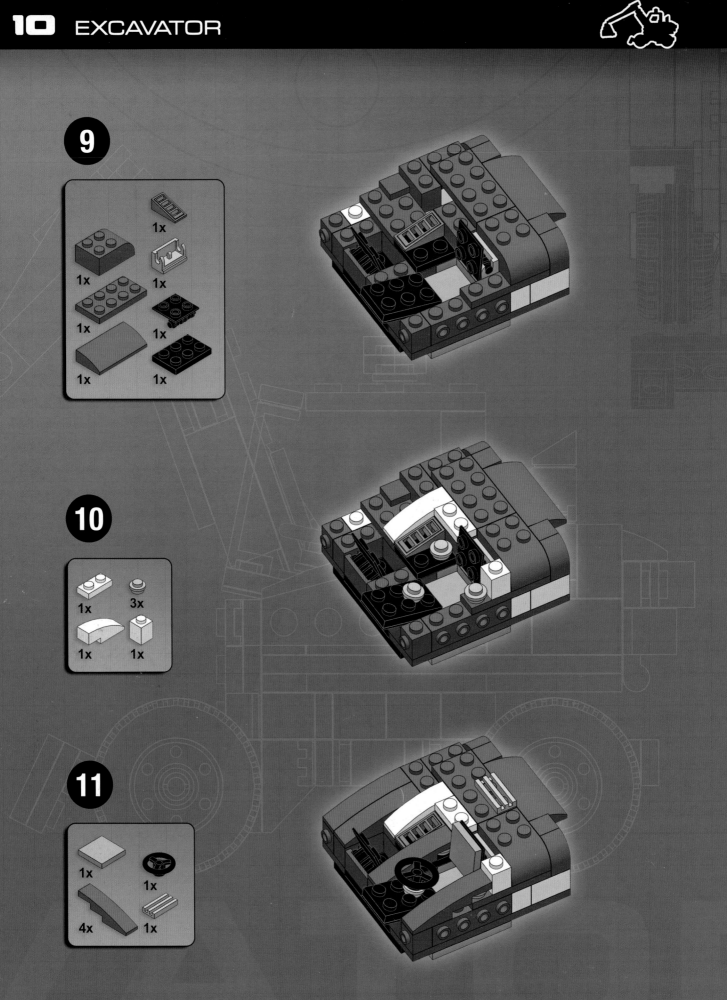

9

1x
1x
1x
1x
1x
1x
1x

10

1x
3x
1x
1x

11

1x
1x
4x
1x

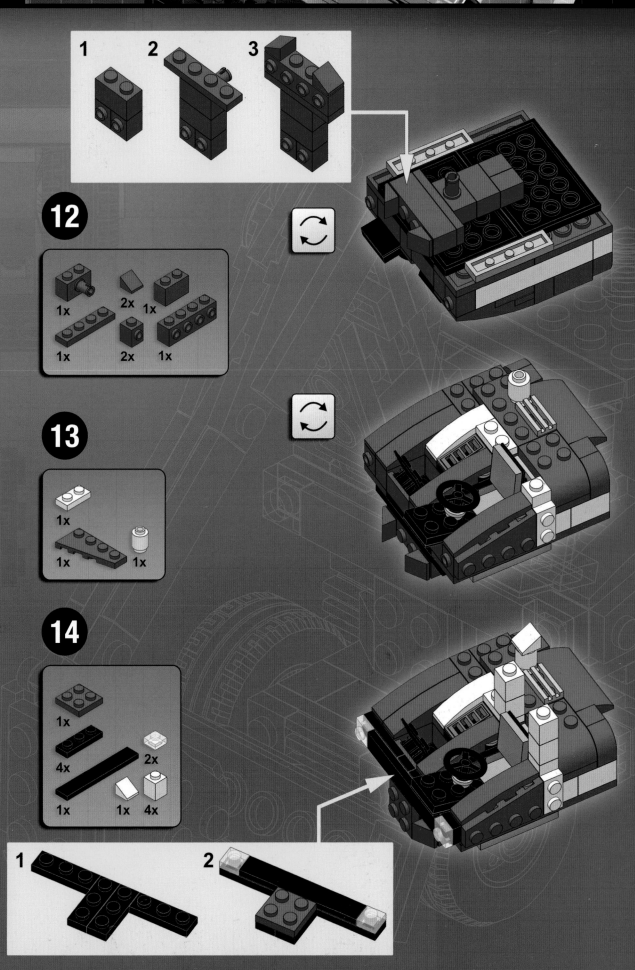

15

1
1x
1x   1x

2
1x
1x   1x

3
1x
1x

4
1x
1x

5
1x

6
1x
1x

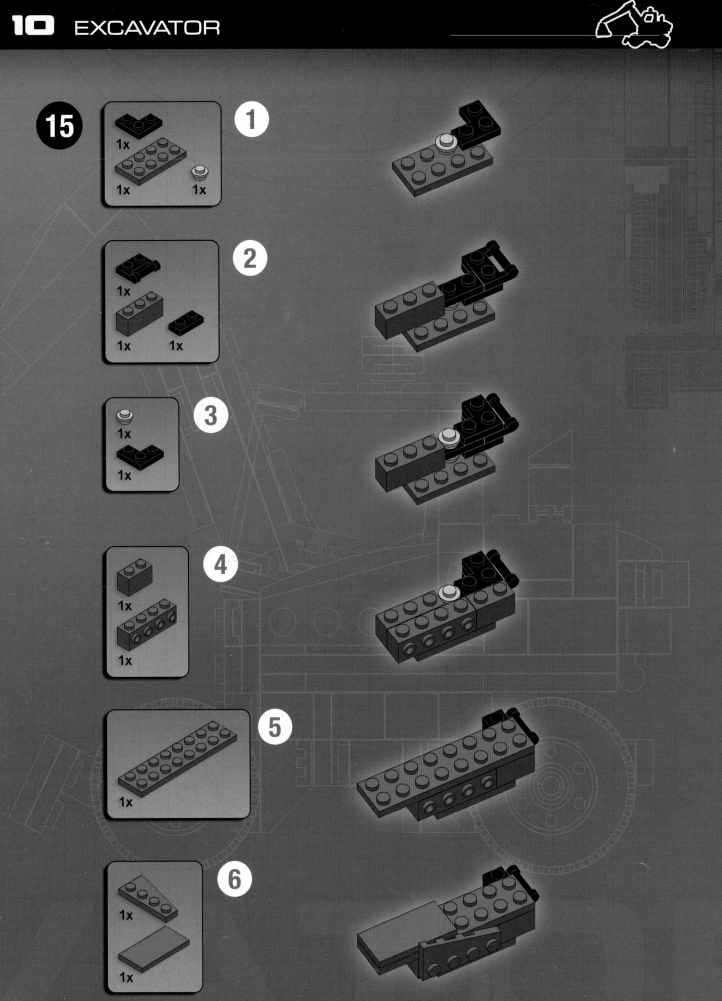

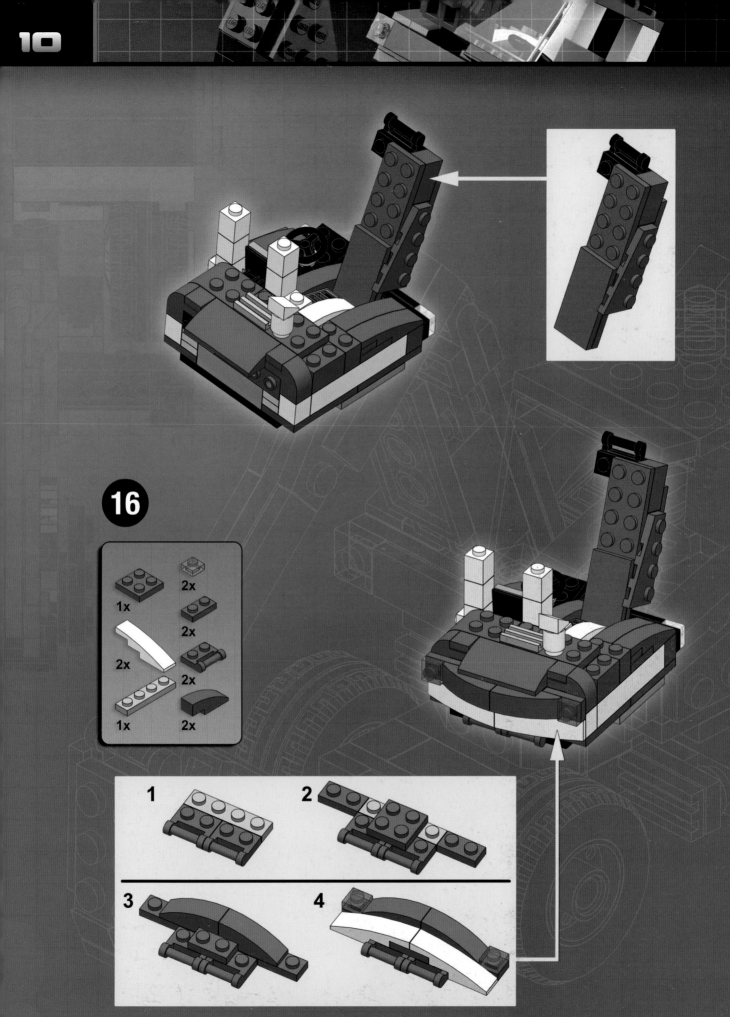

16

1x

2x

2x

2x

1x

2x

2x

1

2

3

4

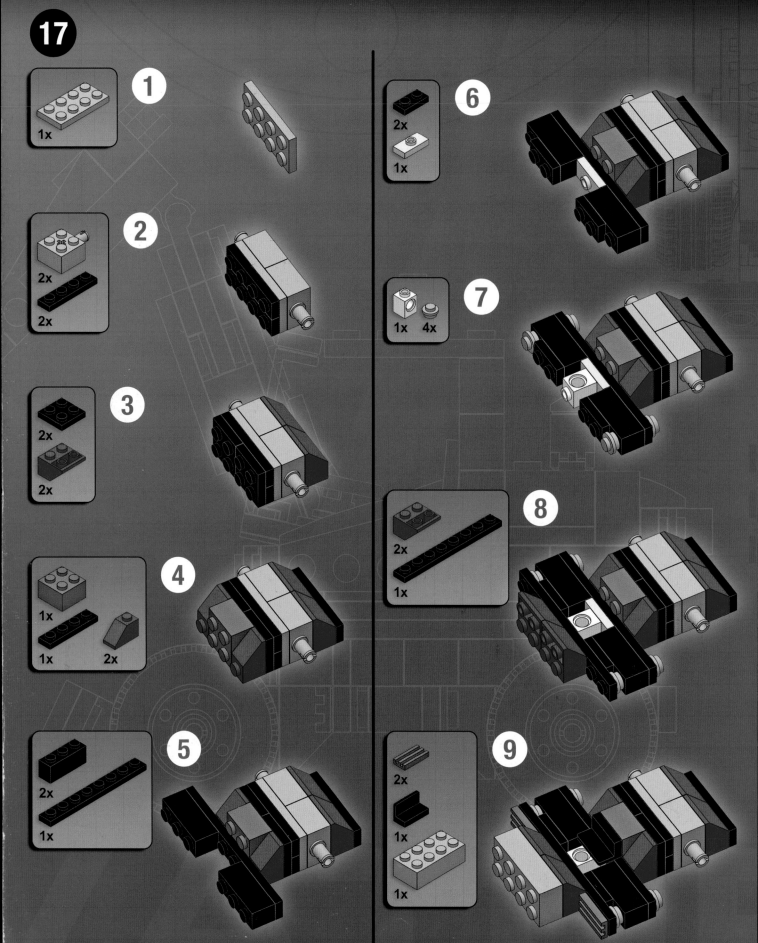

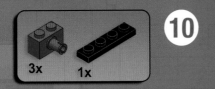

10

11

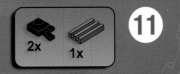

12

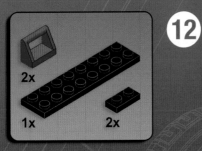

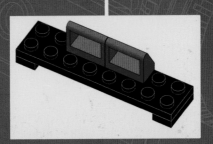

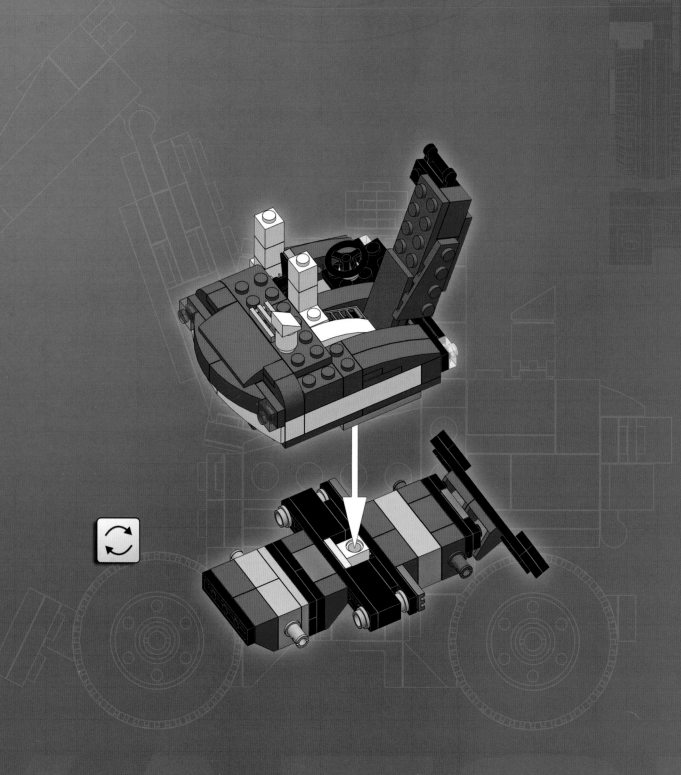

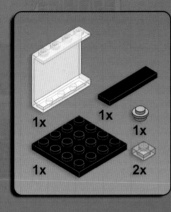

1x 1x 1x 1x 2x

1

2

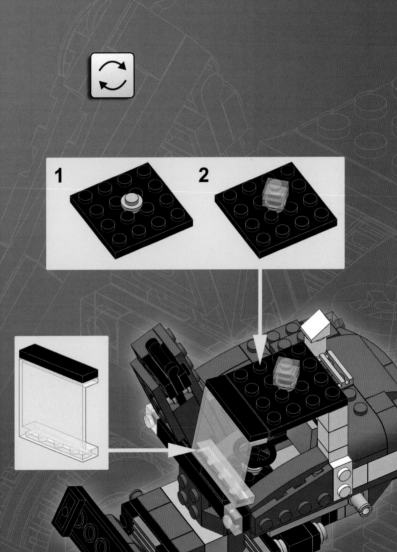

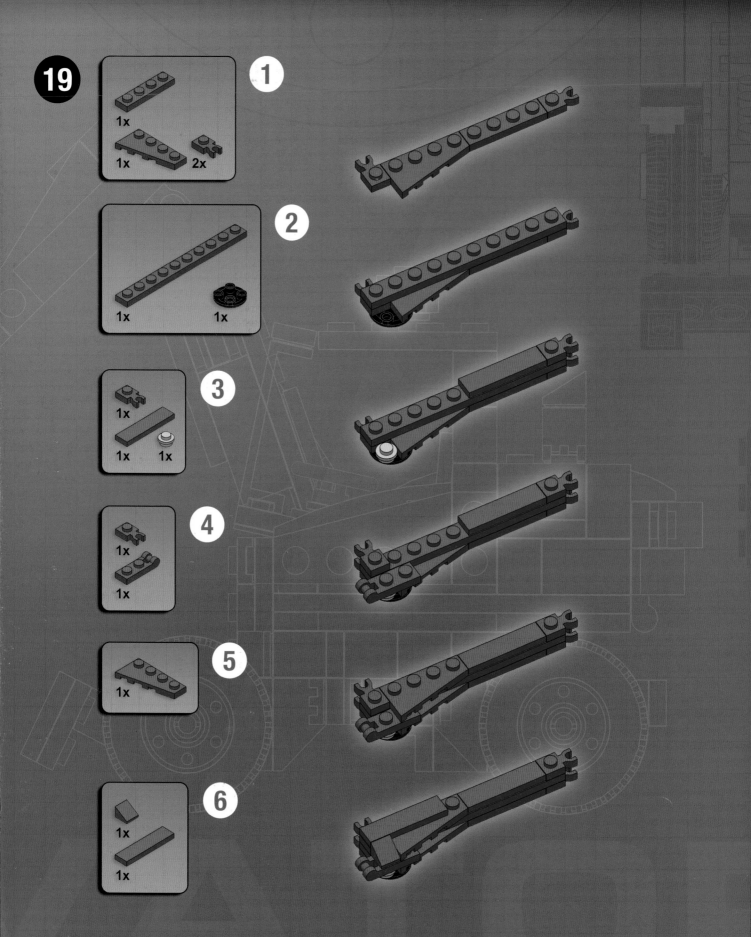

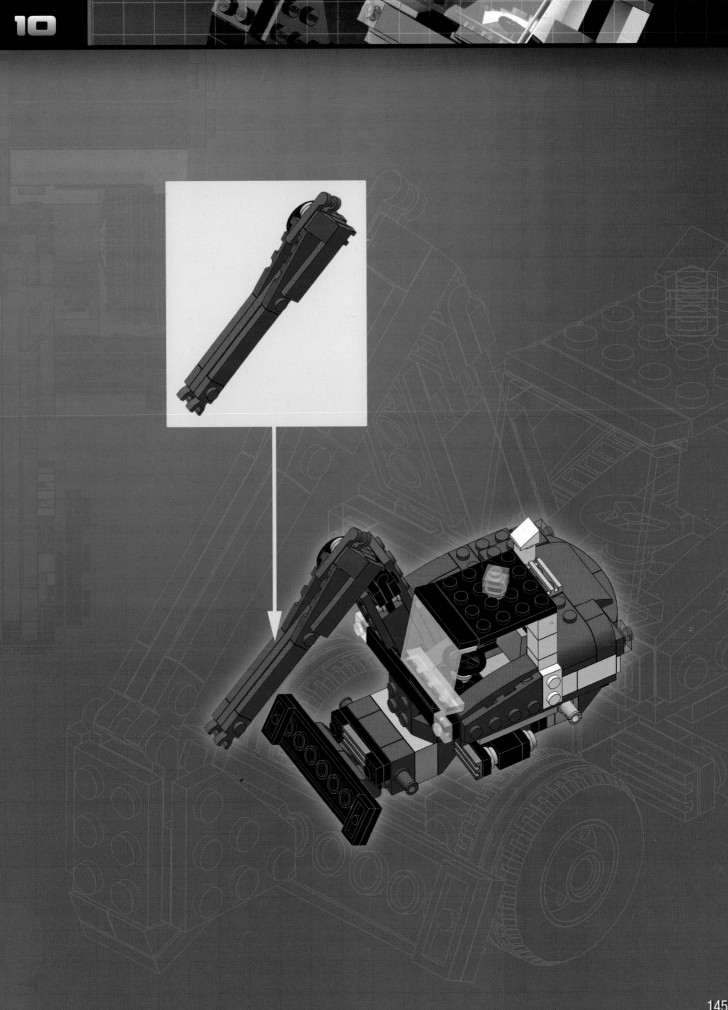

20

 1 1x

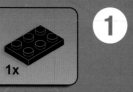 **2** 1x 2x

 **3** 1x 1x 1x

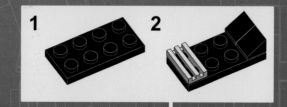
1   2

 **4** 1x / 1x 2x

 **5** 2x

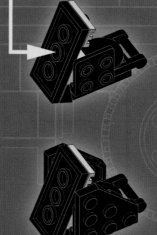

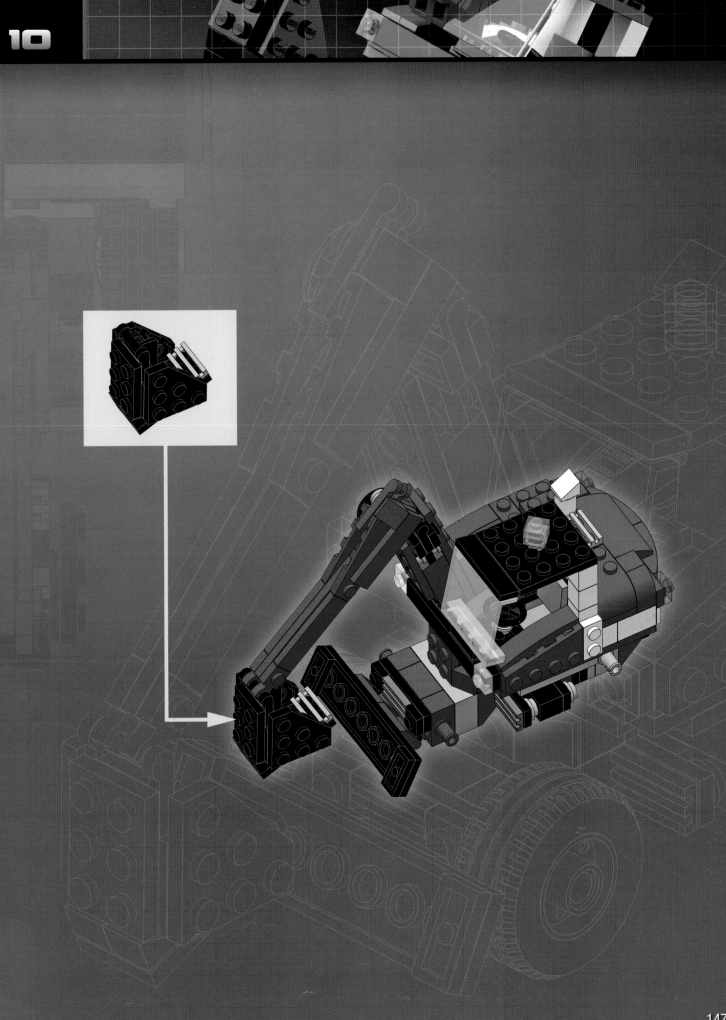

21

4x

4x

UPDATES

Visit *http://nostarch.com/builditvol2* for updates, errata, and other information.